LIVING HAPPILY IN CHINA

LISA CARDUCCI

CHINA
INTERCONTINENTAL
PRESS

图书在版编目（CIP）数据

在中国快乐生活＝Living Happily in China：英文 / （加）李莎著.
—北京：五洲传播出版社，2010. 10

ISBN 978-7-5085-1864-0

I.①在... II.①李... III. ①访华观感－英文 IV. ①D609. 9

中国版本图书馆CIP数据核字(2010)第143945号

Living Happily in China

Author: Lisa Carducci

Photo Credit: Lisa Carducci

Executive Editor: Deng Jinhui

Art Director: Tian Lin

Publisher: China Intercontinental Press

(6 Beixiaomachang, Lianhuachi Donglu, Haidian District,
Beijing 100038, China)

Printer: Beijing sun colour printing co., ltd

Format: 889×1194mm 1/48

Edition: Oct. 2010, 1st edition, 1st print run

Price: RMB 68.00 Yuan

Table of contents

Introduction 1

Chapter 1 Basic secrets 3

Chapter 2 Isn't that odd? 29

Chapter 3 We also act strangely in their eyes 51

Chapter 4 How do the Chinese see us? 63

Chapter 5 It was a good time after all... 71

Chapter 6 Is there anything wrong? 81

Chapter 7 Is integration a kind of cultural prostitution? 87

Conclusion 100

Introduction

The first question is: "Is this possible?" Of course it is! But not all succeed. Let's see why. There are several categories of persons who come to live in China. Some people come as travelers and, once here, they decide that this country is worth being discovered. So, they find a job (sometimes illegally) and settle down. Another group is made up of persons who come to begin a new life after a disastrous relationship. They are fragile and unprepared to adjust to a new lifestyle and mentality. According to unverified sources, 30–50 percent of the expats living and working in China leave before the expected end of their terms. A significant number of them, suffering persistent loneliness, sit watching DVDs and drinking. The third group is made of those who follow their spouses sent to China by their companies or their governments. Not only have they sacrificed their own careers, they may be unable to find positions in China where they can use their skills. They also miss their families and friends, feel an emptiness, frustration, imbalance, a sense of injustice, and loss of identity, and are the most vulnerable to depression, alcoholism, and marital problems. More or less well-prepared, more or less willing to integrate the local population, as well as being trapped by the fact their spouses and children are also here, they may be equipped with many or few survival tools – and I'm talking specifically about the language. The impact of the ability to communicate is greater than one can imagine.

How is it that after two "exploration" trips in the 1980s and almost two decades of life in China, I consider myself perfectly integrated and happy? I will not keep my secrets but share them with you, as living happily in China is worth the effort.

In May 2009, the Association of Italian Women of Beijing invited me to deliver a lecture on this topic. Among the members of the audience were all kinds of non-Chinese: those who wanted to melt into Chinese society and didn't know how, as well as those who were just crossing off an X on their calendars, counting down the days that remained in their suffering. This is when I decided that this little "manual of the newcomer" needed to be written.

▲

Yellow words in the text refer to pictures.

Green words refer to topics.

Purple sentences summarize the content.

Chapter 1

Basic secrets

On my first tourist visit in 1985, I had no opportunity to make mistakes as we were well "framed" by the local and national guides. But I did – and more that I would like to admit – during my three-month stay in 1989 and again after I came by myself to teach in 1991. I learned from my errors. Let me tell you about the first one. The chair I had for the desk in my room seemed similar to many chairs that were stacked outside the cafeteria, but mine was very uncomfortable: the stuffing was old and hollow in the middle. I decided to exchange it with one of those useless (or so I thought) chairs. In fact, they were all numbered, under the responsibility of specific staff, and kept for ceremonies, celebrations, films, etc. A Chinese staff person came to me and, through gestures, made me understand that I could not do that. "Why?" I asked. "*You guiding,*" he said, meaning that permission should be asked. Ignoring at that time that *you guiding* meant "there are regulations," I asked him where Mr. You Guiding's office was, thinking – in my Western way – that knocking directly on the chief's door was better than losing time climbing up the ladder of hierarchy rung by rung and following the Chinese procedure. I was totally wrong.

If it had happened today, I would address the same person this way: "I'm sorry to disturb you, and I know you are very busy. I have a problem with my chair and would like it to be replaced. But I don't know whom to ask for that; would you be kind enough to tell me what to do?" The worker would take this on as a duty and perhaps as an honor to help the foreigner who knows so well how to behave in a Chinese environment and say, "I'll take care of this matter for you." The next day, his superior would enquire about the problem and, in the following days, two workers would deliver a new chair to my room and take away the broken one. I can hear some of you sigh, saying it takes too long, why waste so much time, why are the Chinese so complicated... Don't forget that **you** are in China, and this is the way things are done here. Do you want to be happy or not? It's up to you.

An Italian woman, who is the wife of an ambassador and has been living (happily) in many countries, sees the situation with great wisdom: "Every country has something good," she says. "So I think we must search from the very beginning what is good in a new country, and go along building on this value."

Sure enough, differences impress people more than similarities in a new place, and we are shocked by what doesn't conform to our own habits and to the standards with which we feel very comfortable. We often forget that what is different can also be good – or even better!

I like to say that I live happily in China because

my settling down here came at a moment when I was questioning my life, culture, and religion. So I treated this situation as a blank slate, a *tabula rasa*, then I took one point at a time, examined it, compared it, and decided whether I preferred my own view, the Chinese one, or a totally new one. I don't put a label of my culture today; I just know it fits me perfectly!

Now, pay attention, please. When I say "integration," I don't mean "assimilation." One woman in the audience felt frustrated. She used the word hypocrisy to describe the attitude of a foreigner who "becomes a Chinese." One can keep one's own culture totally, and I would say it is even a duty to spread it among the Chinese who are so eager to know about the Western world. But when it comes to adapting to the host society, we must manage harmoniously with the Chinese way of doing things.

Use your three words and take the bus

People often ask how long it took me to learn Chinese. When I arrived, I could not speak it at all, and my teaching tasks didn't allow me to take classes at the same time. I bought a book written for foreign learners of Chinese with the accompanying cassettes, and I started studying by myself.

The book taught "*Ni hao ma?*" as the most ordinary greeting. But I observed the Chinese around me, and no one used the "*ma*," which is a question, as in "How do you do?" In fact, only foreigners ask,

"Are you okay?" instead of saying "*Ni hao*," meaning literally, "You good" or "I wish you good." This comes from the will of the Chinese to make their language easier for foreign learners. While adapting it to an American form (that ironically is no longer in use), they corrupted it. According to different periods of the day, one can say "*zaoshang hao*" ("morning good"), "*wanshang hao*" ("evening"), etc.

Another example of over-adaptation is the word *Ayi*. *Ayi* means "aunt," but not a blood relative or an aunt by her marriage with your uncle. It is the name a child should call a woman of the same age as his or her mother; this woman may be the ice cream vendor, the maid, or even you, a foreigner, when you meet your Chinese friend with her little boy on the street. But *Ayi* has ended up meaning "maid," and the Chinese, when talking with foreigners, may say, "If you need an *Ayi*, I can recommend a good one," which is a "Chinese-for-foreigners" expression.

It is by using your basic knowledge such as "*Ni hao*," "*Duoshao qian*," "*Xiexie*," and "*Bukeqi*," that you will learn Chinese. Day by day, you will add one or two words, and no matter what, you will make mistakes. Forget about them! When you entered primary school, you started writing and reading simple words long before you mastered the whole alphabet. Do you remember?

You also have to observe what the Chinese do or say in different situations. The culture in which a language was born and that nourishes it can't be learned in textbooks, but in life. And the best places to get an immersion in real life are the market and public transportation.

Dare to take your cotton bag or the basket you bought in South China as a souvenir and go to the market by yourself, whether alone or with company. Dare to take the bus and the subway. It's not by sitting

in the back seat of your black, air-conditioned car with your Chinese driver that you will gain the ability to move in the city and among the people.

Certainly, all will not be perfect from the first try, but you will profit from your mistakes. Let me tell you a story. The first time I wanted to buy eggs, I pointed at some eggs in a box and asked for "*Yi jin*" (500 g). Once at home, I tried to crack the eggs but was surprised at how tough they were. In fact, what I had bought were salted, preserved duck eggs. I had not yet heard of *xian ya dan*. Another day, I went to the market and bought some *you cai* (a kind of cabbage). The merchant used his fingers to indicate "3" as merchants often do with foreigners instead of talking. I gave him 3 Yuan and left. He smiled, said something I didn't understand, then turned to the other vendors in the market and they all laughed together. Only several days later did I realize that I had paid 10 times too much; he'd meant 3 *jiao* (*mao*). Later, I went to a state-owned food store for rice. At the beginning of the 1990s, ration coupons were still necessary for staples such as cereals (including bread, cookies), oil, and meat. Not being a Chinese person with a Beijing *hukou* (residence permit), I had no tickets, but my students used to let me enjoy some they didn't use, as they took their meals at the university cafeteria. Instead of serving me, the woman selling the rice tried to explain something to me that I guessed was "Where did you get these tickets? You are not Chinese, you can't buy." I insisted with gestures, in French, Italian, and English, but I was talking to a wall. Finally, she took me by the sleeve and... threw me out. This is what I thought she was doing

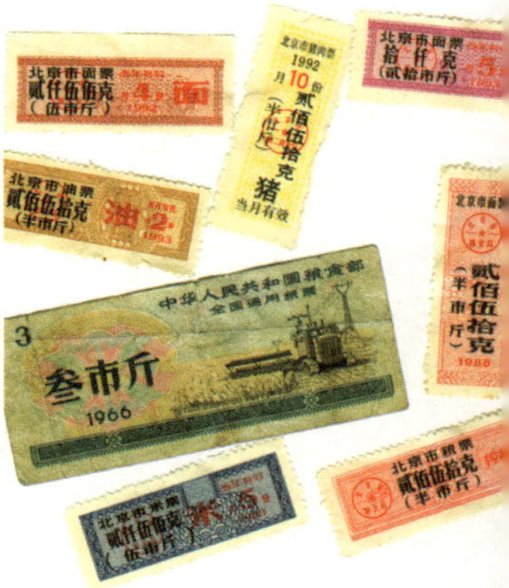

but, in fact, she was indicating a restaurant across the street to me. In short, once more the mistake had been mine. I had asked for *mifan*, which means "steamed rice ready to eat," while she was selling raw rice or *da mi*. Nothing is worth direct experience!

Humility, a major value

We Westerners are certain and proud of ourselves and we like to show it. For the Chinese, humility is one of the deepest moral values. Though things are changing with the young generation, who, for example, are starting to accept a compliment with a smiling "*Xiexie*" instead of protesting that they don't deserve it, it is still very important to never make a Chinese lose face. What does that mean in practical terms? Let's say a clerk has obviously shorted you 10 Yuan. If you say, "Hey, you are cheating me! Quick, give me 10 more," you are done. Instead, if you keep the change displayed and ask, "Did I give you a 100-Yuan bill?" or "How much is the necklace?," taking the "blame" yourself, you will be immediately given your due, with excuses. Never say "you are wrong," but "is it possible that there is a mistake?" I can hear you say that in our Western culture also it's impolite to accuse someone who made a mistake, but why, once in China, do we see so many foreigners behaving as if only they knew and the Chinese were inferior?

I have witnessed a young Canadian woman talking very rudely to a postal employee, while she was responsible for the mistake because of her inadequate Chinese. I had followed the whole conversation and, in front of the blushing operator, I told my Canadian friend that "she" had behaved wrongly.

When you ask for a service or any kind of help, use formulations such as "*Qing bangman*" ("Could you please help me?"), "*Mafan nin*" ("I'm disturbing you"), or

"Ruguo fangbian..." ("When it's convenient for you..."). You will always be welcomed sincerely, because the Chinese can't resist those who are polite. Instead, those who demand to be served will be ignored.

On the one hand, it's due to modesty that the Chinese refuse compliments. On the other hand, they easily compliment others. You need only say, *"Ni hao!"* and they will say, "Your Chinese is very good!" with thumbs up. But they expect you to humbly refuse the compliment, saying *"Nali, nali"* ("Where is that?"), *"Hai cha de yuan"* ("I'm still far from"), or *"Nin guojiang le!"* ("You exaggerate!").

Calling names

We have said something about a child calling a woman of his mother's age *Ayi*. The equivalent for a man is *Shushu* (uncle). If the persons are the age of his grandparents, the child will call them *Yeye* (grandfather) and *Nainai* (grandmother). Polite greetings consist in saying these names respectfully. There is no need to add anything else.

I will never forget – after two or three months in Beijing – when I asked directions of an old man repairing bicycles on a street corner close to the Workers' Stadium. I addressed him, *"Lao Daye, qing gaosu wo..."* The man slowly stood up, put his left hand on his hip, and shaking his right index finger as one does when reprimanding a child, he said (in Chinese), "You called me Old Grandfather?" Looking at his severe expression, I thought I had done something wrong, but he added, "I've been working here for 17 years, and it's the first time a foreigner calls me 'Grandfather.' I'm so glad I have a foreign granddaughter!" Uufff!

But how to address a Chinese colleague, neighbor, employee, doctor, etc.? The Chinese are given a name when they are born. Most of the time, at home will be added a "baby name" that is used only by the family members until the child attends school and even until he or she decides that it's time to choose a proper name. For example, the daughter of Mr. Du was called Du Ma, but she has always been called "Yiyi," meaning "One," as she was born on October 1. Baby names are often a repetition of the same syllable.

You will not call your colleagues Mr. Li or Mrs. Wang, and even less likely by their given names. The Chinese make frequent use of *Lao* and *Xiao* before the family name, according to the age of the person with regard to yours. Lao Li, or Old Li, means that Mr. Li is older than you, while Mrs. Wang, being younger, will be called Xiao Wang or Little Wang. This *lao*, the same as in *lao wai* or "old foreigner" is not offensive. It is very friendly. In your work place, Mr. Chen may be younger than you, but if he is the director, you must recognize his function and call him Chen *zhuren* or "President Chen." Any title must be mentioned when calling a person: Jia *daifu* (Doctor Jia), Wu *laoshi* (Professor Wu), etc. *Laoshi* can be used for men and women to whom you want to show respect. For example, your driver may call you Lan *laoshi*, while you will call him Bao *shifu*. *Shifu* is another all-purpose name meaning literally "master," as the craftsmen used to be referred to in the old times. You can call your driver, the electrician, the car mechanic or the shoe repair woman "*shifu*" (with or without their family names), and they will feel very happy. That means you recognize their skills and appreciate them. Other titles you will probably hear often in your work surroundings are: *laoban* (boss), *lingdao* (chief), *fuzhuren* (vice-president or deputy director), and *jingli* (manager).

There are several words meaning "woman." When you address an envelope to a woman who has no title, you write "Liu *nushi*," meaning Mrs. Liu. If Liu has a respectable age, you will say, orally, "Liu *taitai*." When introducing a woman as the wife of your boss, you will introduce "Liu *furen*." Remember that a Chinese woman doesn't take her husband's name when she marries. Mrs. Liu remains Liu all her life, even after marrying Mr. Gong.

Before the 1990s, the word *Tongzhi* (comrade) was an easy catch-all name for everyone. But this word has nowadays taken the meaning of "homosexual" and is no longer used for other people. Westerners are often reluctant to call a restaurant waitress *Fuwuyuan* (literally servant or service person) and used to call them *Xiaojie* (or Miss). But this word also has changed meaning and now refers to the "*San Pei*" or "Three accompaniments" – beauties who make lonely men happy in bars and hotels. In fact, *Fuwuyuan* has no derogatory meaning in Chinese. It's the right name for this function.

Now you can understand why the Chinese are

so eager to know your *age*: they must situate you compared to themselves. Even when they call you intimately "sister," for example, they want to know if you are their big sister (*jiejie*) or little sister (*meimei*), as these words are different in Chinese.

Finally, the best way not to make mistake is to ask the counterpart, "How should I address you?" This is what the Chinese do when they ask you, "*Wo zenme chenghu nin?*" (*Nin* is you (*ni*) when showing respect, like *Vous, Usted,* or *Lei* in French, Spanish, and Italian.)

To ask politely a Chinese person his or her name, one should say, "*Nin gui xing?*" This means literally "Your precious surname?" So, being modest as the Chinese rules command, your interlocutor will answer, "*Mian gui, xing X,*" this is "Forget the precious, my surname is X." It would be good to learn the question as well as the answer, since you can find yourself on both sides of the situation.

As always, with regard to names, it may happen that you are certain you registered somewhere, but your name can't be found on a list. This is how it happened to me once, at the check-in for a flight, when I was not on the passenger list between the Bs and the Ds. One may panic in such moments... As Westerners used to give their name in the order of given name-surname, the Chinese often fill forms or registrations in this order. They are not to be blamed. Can you always detect what is the family name and what is the given name in Arabic, Romanian, Senegalese, or Thai language? Even my Yahoo page says, "Hello Carducci!" to me...

Open your eyes as large as you can

When in Rome, do as the Romans do, the proverb says. It's by observing – and using – little gestures, acts, and habits that you will insert yourself into the Chinese community and be accepted by the Chinese. Have you noticed that the Chinese always hand out their business cards and take yours with two hands? If you are over 45, you probably remember that when you were a child, you were taught to use your right hand, as being left-handed was considered abnormal, and using both hands together, childish. But, for the Chinese, using two hands means that they consider they are holding something very precious. A name card is something precious as it contains all kinds of personal information such as your official name, your title(s) and functions, and the numbers where you can be reached. Some Chinese have a common business card and a personal business card.

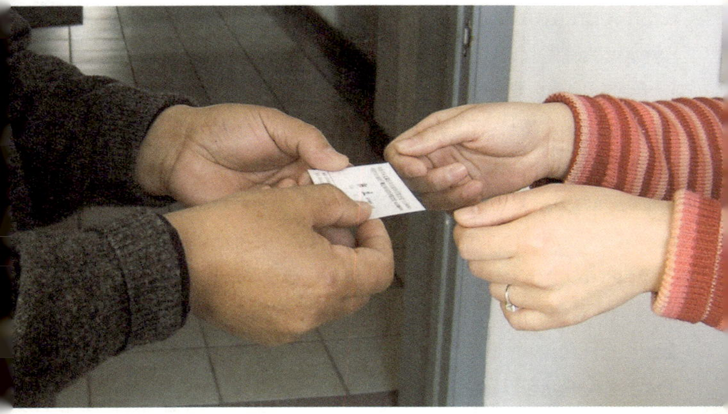

The right way to introduce yourself is by offering your name card. Always have a good provision of cards when you go out. If you don't have a name card to give, you should apologize and not treat it as something trivial. A name card is like a part of oneself. It should be given and received with two hands. It's convenient to read it when you get it. Comment on the "quality" of the person whom it represents; say something flattering about the information. Never throw or "forget" on the table a name card that has been given to you. It would be a huge insult to the one who has honored you with such friendship.

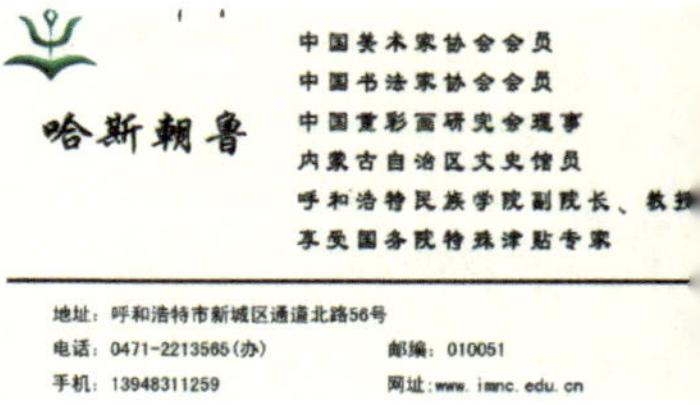

While I write this, I remember how impersonal China was not so long ago. Not only there were no author's name on several books, that had been written on order, by and for a work unit, but an art show was announced this way, in *China Daily*, for instance: "A painting exhibition by a famous artist will open on May 5"; "... Symphonic Orchestra directed by a foreign maestro..." I often heard my Chinese colleagues saying on the telephone, "I'm CCTV Overseas Programs," or "I'm Foreign Languages University." No name. What was important was the unit (*danwei*) and, if someone wanted to investigate further, the function. Not the individual.

The Chinese make an easy use of the words "friend" and "friendship." The president of the state calls each citizen a friend in his New Year's speech. The TV anchors call the audience, whom they have never seen, friends. The chief of a remote village calls all "visitors from afar," friends. If you rent your garage to a Chinese person, you become his friend. We can have another understanding of friendship in our culture, but it is important to know what this means for the Chinese people around us.

In the 1980s, Westerners coming to China were strictly told not to tip the Chinese. Some did, just to see what would happen. A restaurant waiter or waitress would protest while blushing, and the establishment's manager would come to the table to explain that Chinese don't accept tips. Tour guides were offered a "gift" brought from the tourists' country, but not money. As taxis at that time were not numerous and were too expensive for the local population, they were reserved for foreigners, who were obliged to pay in FECs (foreign exchange

certificates). As they were often given tips, the drivers were the first Chinese to finally accept them, but not wait for them. The hotel restaurants for foreigners followed.

The Chinese never refuse a service you ask of them, because fulfilling a favor to someone is making a friend. But how do you show your appreciation, if giving money is offensive? In fact, when you accept someone's help, you become indebted to this person. It would be easier to pay and forget it, wouldn't it? At any moment, a Chinese person who did you a favor may come to you and ask you to do something for him. What, exactly? Perhaps picking up his little girl at school on a day he can't, or using your "foreign power" as a sponsor for a visa from your country. Certain requests may be very hard to refuse and may even be beyond your capacities. If you owe something to a Chinese person, be aware that this delicate situation may occur, and your answer may decide the future of your relationship.

If for a reason or another you must refuse a service, never say, "I can't." Say "This is very difficult, but for a friend like you, I will do my best!" Doing your best may mean finding the person who can help. But do it!

In a way to show your gratitude for a service, you can offer a *hong bao* or red envelope containing money to the child of the family. This will be well-received. You can also bake a cake, which you will offer in whole, not just one piece. You can buy a green plant, if the family has enough space for it, or fruit that is still expensive at the beginning of the season. But avoid offering such gifts immediately after you have received the service, which would too obviously show that you are repaying the favor, thus implying that you don't accept the friendly relationship which has been created by it.

On the Chinese Lunar New Year (Spring Festival), people of the same generation usually don't exchange presents. When children pay a visit to their elder relatives to wish them a happy New Year, they generally receive a red envelope containing money. The New Year's money is called *yasuiqian*, a Chinese word meaning "to crush the evil spirits" and this gift expresses the hope that the children remain safe during the New Year.

Around the table

There is much to say in this chapter and much to learn around a table. I could say that in China, all important discussions, contracts, and decisions happen around the table. The urban Chinese have been living until recently in small houses, where it was not comfortable to invite guests, so they would invite them to a restaurant.

Most restaurants, even the modest ones, have *baojian* or private rooms, where only the waitresses, standing beside the table, will hear all of the conversation. The guests can drink, laugh, sing, eat, and make all the noise they want. A noisy dinner is a successful dinner for the Chinese.

Let's enter the room, where there is a round table, generally for eight, ten, or twelve guests. (The Chinese try to avoid odd numbers of guests.) Generally, the most honorable guest sits to the right of the host, who faces the door, and the second guest in importance sits at his left. Never choose a place by yourself – even if you are obviously the main guest – instead, wait to be told where to sit. If the host says *Suibian*, that means "as you wish" but, even then, wait to be indicated a place, as – being a foreigner – you are probably the main guest or one of the guests.

Facing the host or the main guest is the "second" or

the assistant of the host, who, the closest to the door, will be able to leave easily to pay the bill, to move easily to call for service, or to receive a late guest. The other guests will sit *suibian*, and you will notice that they don't alternate man and woman as we often do in the West. Maybe smokers will stick together or old friends who have not seen each other for a while will sit next to each other.

When it comes to ordering the dishes, there are two ways. The host will order himself, while asking for suggestions, or the menu will pass from hand to hand and each guest will order a dish, according to what has been ordered by the others before. The setting of a menu is a very complex operation that requires paying attention to the four tastes (sweet, salty, bitter, spicy), to the colors, and to the texture for a well-balanced menu. Young Chinese – let's say, under 45 – are generally unaware of this cultural aspect of a meal.

The table is set before the guests arrive and, according to what beverages are ordered, the waitresses will collect and bring back a series of glasses that will not be useful. But sometimes, beer or milk will be served in a wine glass. When they have foreign guests, the Chinese often order *putaojiu* (literally "grape alcohol" or wine), but this is for the toasts that will follow one another, not to accompany the meal. So you will be asked again what you want to drink! The wine or the *baijiu* that is served is not for quenching your thirst. Don't drink alone, as this would be impolite. If you are thirstier than the others, then propose a toast yourself. The Chinese expect this from

their foreign guests.

Cold dishes will start to arrive, and wine will be served. You can sip your "welcoming" tea as you wish but don't start to eat and drink alcohol before the signal is given. The signal will be given by the host to the most important guest, probably you. You must take a piece of the dish that is in front of you, then the Lazy Susan will start to turn. Normally, you should taste every dish. You can take two or three servings of what you prefer, but only when the dish passes before you. Don't turn the Lazy Susan yourself. And never take a plate into your hand to serve yourself or another person.

Since 2003, when the SARS epidemic hit China, restaurants started to add a pair of chopsticks or a spoon for service to each dish. But some persons, including me, who often forget, continue to use their own chopsticks for serving. It's an old habit, and in fact not so terrible, as the chopsticks should not touch the mouth, but only bring a piece of meat or vegetables close to the mouth for the lips or teeth to grasp the food.

It is polite to serve the best pieces to your neighbor, but this habit is no longer compulsory, especially in the presence of foreigners. You can't tell your host, "We are not used to that," but a Chinese person among the diners may say it, as the Chinese are getting used to dine in company of non-Chinese. However, if you are served something you dislike, just show gratefulness for the care that is taken of you and leave the food on your plate. The plates are regularly changed for clean ones during the dinner, so the food you have not yet eaten will be taken away. But if you are served a whole crab, or other expensive food that you prefer not to eat, you can offer it to others saying you are allergic, or forbidden to eat it, and adding that you understand this is too expensive to waste.

What about slurping soup or tea? All Chinese know (and say it) that Westerners consider this as being not so polite. They add that it's not polite for the Chinese also, especially in the presence of foreigners. But they still do it. Let me tell you that, after many years in China, I started to slurp liquids automatically and do it with pleasure if I'm alone. My interpretation is that the old Chinese habit came naturally, but is based on scientific reasons: when slurping tea, the drinker absorbs air together with the liquid, and a chemical reaction influences the taste of the tea. Soup goes drunk in China; the reason for slurping soup is probably the same, and the habit persists even when "eating" soup with a spoon.

Have you noticed that the Chinese never ask or say

"to like/not to like" about food or drinks but "to be used to." This is the way of refusing something, saying "*Wo bu tai xiguan*" ("I'm not used to it"). Ironically, *xiguan* is close to *xihuan*, which means "to like." If you are asked "*Ni xiguan Zhongguo cai?,*" give yourself a chance by saying something like China has a great culinary tradition, and you have not yet discovered all of it.

It will not be long before you will be invited to *ganbei* (literally "dry the glass"). If you – man or woman – go "bottoms up" from the first toast, you will have no margin later to say you can't drink. Even if you like the *bai jiu* (white liquor) and can absorb a certain quantity of it, you better protect yourself by saying you are not used to drinking, or you had an operation recently, or you are under medication. It is acceptable to drink only a drop, without *ganbei*, which is not refusing to drink. If you really can't take alcohol, you can *ganbei* with tea or juice. When the Chinese have a foreign guest, they often order an expensive bottle of red or white wine. As China is not a "wine culture" several of the Chinese will add ice cubes to their wine, or sugar to dry wine, which they consider bitter. In fact, the Chinese *gan hong* (dry red) are a little sweet in a way to adapt to the Chinese taste. If you see ice or sugar on the table, watch for the moment when they will put some in your own glass, and prevent them from doing so, explaining that you prefer to take your wine naturally. If they pressure you to *ganbei* with wine, you can say kindly that this wine is very high quality, and you would prefer to sip it slowly, enjoying its taste fully. Doing so, you contribute to the "wine culture education." But you must toast... So, ask for permission to have only a mouthful or, in extreme cases, to replace the *bai jiu* or the wine with another beverage.

Here, I must confess what I did in 1993. I was part of a group of five foreigners who were invited to Jinan by a magazine to which we had cooperated. The first evening, the American woman sitting at my right accepted toasts and even proposed toasts, as she liked to drink so much, but the next morning she could not get out of bed. There were two men who both had stomach problems and a Northern European woman who had never taken alcohol. At lunch, the second day, I was sitting at the right of the mayor, and I did my best to save the reputation of the foreigners. I had a bottle of liquor filled with water, and, after each toast, when I had a chance, I filled my small glass, but obviously not the mayor's. Sometimes he filled both glasses, and I was obliged to drink. I think we were up to nine *ganbei* when the mayor realized that this foreign woman besides him was "*tai lihai*" (too strong). He sniffed my... water, and discovered he had been cheated. He was really angry and I can understand him. He ordered another bottle and kept it in his hand, not giving me a chance to rest between two *ganbei*, and I had maybe four or five in a row. I prayed that I would not get drunk, which is for me one of the most disgraceful states of being. The dinner over, my two foreign male companions helped me, as I was "walking on the clouds," down to the door and to the car. In

fact, I still had my head on my shoulders and saved face. Moreover, I saved face for the whole group of Westerners.

You have probably noticed that when a waiter or waitress or a neighbor at the table fills someone's glass or tea cup, a gesture is made, consisting of knocking on the table with two knuckles. Here is the story. An emperor was tired of his living situation, always closed in his palace and deprived of freedom. He decided to travel and see how ordinary people lived. But he could not escape from the hundreds of servants and guards who used to accompanied him. So he traded disguises with his aide. In the evening, while eating in a small local restaurant, the emperor played his role and served tea to the fake emperor. The aide wanted to fall on his knees and kowtow to the emperor, but couldn't. For fear of being discovered if he spoke, he closed his right hand, stuck out the second and third fingers which he bent to represent a pair of knees, and knocked on the table in the position of a person kowtowing. This way he could show respect to his emperor without revealing his disguise. Today, the gesture – that has been simplified – is used to say "thank you" especially if a person is talking and doesn't want to interrupt the flow of conversation.

Chinese dinners start at a signal and also end at a signal. When the host deposits his chopsticks, it's not polite to continue eating. When – usually with the last *ganbei* – he thanks the guests for having "enlightened the evening with their presence" the dinner is over, and it's compulsory to get up and leave. Some Chinese may remain in the room, maybe asking the waiters to pack the leftovers (*dabao*) to be carried away – a habit that I really appreciate, instead of wasting food.

If, during a meal, you have to leave because of another obligation, for example, the proper thing to say is: "*Man man chi*," meaning, "Continue to eat," "Don't mind I have to leave," or "Have fun without me." But you can't leave the table before the end if you are the guest of honor.

When you are invited for dinner by a Chinese family, you are not invited to spend the whole evening there. So, after dinner, you should thank them for the invitation, offer praise again (though you have done so each time a new dish was brought to the table) to the hostess or the cook, and make a motion as if you are leaving. If the hosts have intentions of enjoying your presence longer, they will insist that you stay a little longer and invite you to sit in the living room. If they don't insist, you must leave.

Westerners often offer to wash the dishes and put the dining room in order when they have dinner at a friend's house. This is strange to the Chinese. Maybe you have been surprised that your Chinese guests left immediately after the dinner when you invited them at your place. They did just what they had to do out of politeness. Maybe they were surprised that you did not protest their departure. Next time you know what to do.

Chapter 2

Isn't that odd?

Many things that the Chinese do may seem incorrect to us because we don't understand the cultural reasons that underlie these actions. This is where different mentalities come into conflict, and this is an aspect of what is often called culture shock. The French writer and philosopher Montaigne wrote: « *Chacun appelle barbarie ce qui n'est pas de son usage, comme de vray, il semble que nous n'avons autre mire de la vérité et de la raison que l'exemple et idées des opinions et usances du païs où nous sommes.** » (Montaigne, *Essais*, Livre I, chap. XXXVI, « Des cannibales », p. 203.) Let's see some points together.

Hot or cold?

The first time I came to China in 1985 was with a group. Every two hours we stopped in special halls where tourists were offered tea. Hot tea. It was July and the coldest weather we had in a month was 30

---

* "One calls barbarism what is not of one's use, and it seems that we don't have any other pattern of truth and reason but the example and ideas of opinions and customs of the country where we are."

degrees (Celsius). Most of my travel mates found it ridiculous to be served hot tea on a warm day. But I thought there might have been a reason. In fact, if you heat the inside of your body when it's warm outside, it will not react like it does when you fill it with ice water. In Heilongjiang Province where the temperature drops to –30°C in the winter, ice cream establishments are crowded with customers for the same reason: balancing the internal and external temperature.

In China, plain water is normally served hot – the same hot water that they have just boiled for tea, but without tea leaves – unless you specifically ask for ice cubes in it, which has become possible in recent years because flocks of tourists have brought a new tradition from the outside world. In fact, it's not a healthy practice.

Beer is often preferred at room temperature by Chinese drinkers while most of non-Chinese like it *bing* (iced).

The young generation of Chinese, who now all have a fridge at home and money to buy cold bottled drinks, do as their Western contemporaries and drink frozen drinks. They don't even know how comfortable one can feel when drinking hot liquids on a hot day.

Too fast food

Westerners, Europeans mostly and Italians more than others, go to restaurants not for the meal first but as an outing with friends. So, taking time to chat is as important as eating. They don't expect to be served

before they have had a bit of conversation.

When you enter a Chinese restaurant, there may be a double row of nice girls wearing a *qipao*, who welcome you saying, "*Huanying guanglin*," which means "Your presence is welcomed here." Let's mention that the character for *guang* in this sentence is the one for "light," meaning that your visit brings light to their place. Before you pass between two rows of greeters a hostess will take you in her charge, asking how many persons compose your group, and will find you or ask one of her staff to find you a suitable table, be it in a smoking or non-smoking section. Here, let me remind you not to go seeking a table by yourself.

Sometimes, you have not yet sit down that you are asked what you will eat. This is because some sections of the restaurants are reserved for some specialties, such as hot pot, which requires special tables.

But, in any case, we will be followed by a waitress with her pad and pen, ready to take your order before you look at the menu, before you ask your friends whether they have already tasted this or that dish, and certainly before giving you time to exchange former amusing experiences about eating in Chinese restaurants. If you have recently arrived in China, you will probably feel pedestrian the waiters' haste to take your order. But they were taught this because, for the Chinese, it's important to concentrate all attention and service on the honorable guests to show them how they are valued.

I remember once in Italy with a Chinese friend from China. We had been talking for at least half an hour in a Bologna restaurant when my friend said, "Let's go to another place." "What? You don't like it here?" I asked innocently, as everything seemed fine to me. "They don't care for us," he said, surprised and disappointed. "Oh! We have not yet called the waiter," I remembered. I had forgotten to explain that to him.

Who sits?

Once, on a crowded Beijing bus, I gave my seat to an old man who seemed to have problems balancing while standing. Instead of sitting down, he called his 6-year-old grandson who was behind him and made the fat little emperor sit. I was enraged! The grandfather even kept the boy's schoolbag in his arms!

I often see a woman letting her husband sit instead of sitting herself, but this is their choice and I don't find it shocking.

Often, the Chinese must be told by the bus controller to leave their seat to an elderly person, man or woman, but they don't need to be told that a child is standing; they offer their seat immediately. What I find strange is that the father or the mother could sit and take the child on their laps – making the seat more useful – but they don't.

The old Confucian culture prescribes: "Respect the elders, love the youth." And it is in reference to this rule that the Chinese let the children sit first. And Mao Zedong said that "Women hold half of the sky." So we must not be surprised by the equality between genders in China.

"Ladies first" belongs to the Western culture, and all Chinese people, even the uneducated, have heard this sentence and can repeat it in English. Once, I was coming back from abroad with two suitcases. On the bus were workers from outside Beijing. Four of them prepared to get off at the same stop as I, and I stood in the lineup behind them, handling my heavy suitcases and hoping that they would be kind enough to help me with them. Suddenly, one shouted to me – a foreigner and a woman – "Ladies first!" They all laughed excitedly and changed places to line up behind me, letting me get off alone, with no one to help me with my luggage.

The "Ladies first" concept doesn't apply in Chinese restaurants, where elderly are served before younger guests according to their social rank, not their gender. A man doesn't open a door for a woman because she is a woman, but perhaps because she carries a child, and a woman holds the door to an elderly person because of his or her age.

I must say I'm unhappy with the civil education the young generation receives today. If children always need their parents to remind them to greet a person and how to greet a person they encounter, without their parents when they take the subway, they usually seem to forget to heed the signs over their heads: "Seats reserved to the elderly, disabled, pregnant women, and parents with a child." I don't expect that students, glued to their electronic games or their cell phones, leave their seats to me because I'm a woman (I mean in China), still less because I'm a foreigner, but because of my age. Well, maybe it's only that I don't show it?

Privacy, you said?

It has been long known in the West that there is no Chinese word for privacy. In a Chinese family, everything belongs to everyone, the secrets as well as the stories. When a Chinese person visits a foreigner, he or she may take a letter that is left on a desk and read it without any hesitation. Or take your wedding photo album (they are fond of pictures!) and look at it without asking.

Well, this was very common behavior 20 years ago, and I taught my students not to do that with Westerners. The Chinese who have contact with foreigners have probably attended foreign languages classes and had foreign teachers who told them this as well. So, nowadays, the Chinese are aware. But refraining from looking at things that we feel are personal is still not natural to them.

On the other hand, many non-Chinese friends told me that they find difficult to make friends with Chinese people because "they never speak about themselves, their family members, their thoughts and feelings." This is true. In the last ten years I have conducted interviews of over 200 Chinese people for articles and books. I always face the same reaction: they are willing to talk enthusiastically about their work, but not about their childhood, their relationship with their family members, their matrimonial situation, their wishes, their hobbies, and their hidden talents. They consider that things concerning their own lives are private matters and of no interest in terms of sharing with the public.

Where-are-you-from-what's-your-name-how-old-are-you?

These are the first questions children learn to ask when they start studying English. Unfortunately, they are not told how, when, and whom they should ask.

After so many years in China, I often feel strange to say I'm from Canada, because I have not kept track and am no longer aware of what is going on there.

Inside China, I am often mistaken for a Uyghur by the Uyghur themselves, who address me in their language. More and more Han Chinese ask me to which ethnic minority I belong, and when I jokingly say that I am Kazakh, Kirgiz, or Uyghur, they never doubt me.

Name and nationality questions – though the answer has no importance – are usually well-received by non-Chinese. On the contrary, the age issue is not welcomed. Children ask only because they know how to say this sentence; adults ask in order to situate you in their mental schema so that they can choose the right appellation and the right behavior toward you, as we have seen before.

When my mother came to China along with my daughter and my granddaughters, we were "four generations under a roof," a saying that all Chinese know and a situation they consider as the pinnacle of family happiness. A banquet was offered by CCTV where I was working then, and a speech was addressed in Chinese and translated by one of my colleagues. The translator should have known that in Western culture, old age is not considered a privilege or a grace as it is in China. Every time she repeated "the old lady" in her translation, my mother was shocked and she didn't wait till the end of the speech to ask me why she was being treated so badly when it became clear to her that "she" was the *lao taitai*.

If being asked your age still disturbs you, you can return the question to the one who asked, or invite the asker to guess, and sometimes you can get away without really answering. A woman from the United States, in her 60s, used to joke that she was 108 (a sacred number in Buddhism), and she was granted many compliments on her good health and they wished to her still more longevity.

When I was 42, every single day I was asked my age by an old Chinese woman resting in the sun at the gate of our campus. I always said, "*sishi'er*" – the truth – till the day I mistakenly turned 42 into 24, "*ershisi*" which seemed to satisfy the old lady who thought I was finally telling the truth. From that day I understood that we are the age we look or feel, and I decided that age was only a way to start a conversation, just like the former "What time is it, please?" that the Chinese used, one generation earlier, to approach a foreigner.

Flowers

When I ask Chinese friends about when the Chinese started to pin bouquets on the guests' jackets or dresses (or pin them on themselves) on special occasions such as the opening of a congress, the inauguration of a museum, an art preview, etc., no one remembers; they did not pay attention to this when

it was new. But looking at old pictures or movies, I would say it started in the 1980s – which means after the beginning of reform and opening up of China. And I see an obvious Western influence there. But the idea has been "partially" imported. I'll explain two main points. In the West, men usually receive a carnation, and women, a rose. Orchids are kept for very special occasions, while in China, they are common flowers, easy to cultivate or to buy, and they are used for both genders. The second point is the size of the bouquet, which goes from "discreet" in the West to "garden-size" in China.

It is also quite new for the Chinese to bring flowers to a hospitalized person, to offer fresh flowers to the hostess on a visit, or to a person who celebrates his or her birthday. If in the West men seldom get fresh flowers as a gift, the Chinese don't make a gender difference. Same for flowers offered to a classical singer or to actors.

I remember that toward the end of the last century, media often mentioned that the Chinese life conditions had improved enough to offer people the possibility of buying fresh flowers to take home for no special reason. This was seen as a sign of economic and social progress.

Dior in pajamas

If you were living in Beijing before the 21st century, you can't have forgotten the famous Silk Market. It was then in a narrow alley close to the Friendship Store and was a kind of "institution" for foreign tourists.

At the time, it really sold silk and only silk. Foreign visitors used to ask for silk pajamas, but the vendors didn't know what they were talking about. Even if these foreigners could have spoken Chinese, they wouldn't know how to say "pajamas" in Chinese, and neither would their Chinese friends, as the Chinese were used to sleep in their underwear. One day, a word appeared: *shuiyi*. What's more logical and simple than this combination of "sleep" and "clothe"?

As sleeping wear, pajamas are a Western creation. As there was demand, Chinese manufacturers put the *shuiyi* on the market. Not long after, the Chinese started to buy pajamas, too, and, finding them very comfortable, they wore them to go out! You could see an old man walking in a park in his cotton pajamas printed with teddy bears, a middle-aged woman with make-up and jewels shopping at the supermarket in her pink pajamas dotted with red hearts, or a slim

20-year-old girl licking an ice cream cone, in pajamas, at the bus stop. It was so natural for the Chinese that they didn't understand the mockery of a cartoon illustrating one of my books: A man wearing pajamas at the vegetable market is looked down on by a surprised foreign woman. He addresses her saying: "So what? It's a Christian Dior!"

As there are so many pajama-wearing Chinese people out in public, several Westerners don't find it odd anymore (only a little funny) and think it's a Chinese fashion. When in the hospital, pajamas are your uniform, your ID card. You have to wear them all the time, even if you take a walk to enjoy fresh air (which patients in Western hospitals are generally

not allowed to do). Often, a patient has to go from his room in building 8 to building 5 for a blood test, then to building 9 for a heart check, and in between, to building 2 to feed the cashier, and at the end to building 4 to get medicine. Wearing the hospital pajamas allows him to move about freely. I have experienced the situation myself.

One year before the Shanghai World Exhibition 2010, the host municipality started a campaign to uproot this "wild" practice. Opinions were controversial, as some – mostly foreigners – found it cute and ingenious. I think that the Chinese adopted a Western piece of clothing but they changed its signification and use. These are "their" pajamas, and they wear them for their own purpose. It doesn't harm anyone, just like another common practice in Shanghai: putting the clothes to dry in the sun on long poles that jutted over the streets, a habit that was also considered "wild" and odd by the local government.

This is my gift for you

Would you believe that there are Chinese aged 30 to 40 who don't know the date on which they were born? Their parents don't remember, either. But they remember that their son was born in the year of the Ox, in the summer, and their daughter, the year of the Sheep, at the beginning of spring. Even birthdays follow the wave of globalization, and children who enter school must have a birthday like their fellow Westerners. If their parents remember precisely that the child was born on the 6th day of the Fifth Lunar month, they can easily find that the date corresponded that year to the 14th of June, for example. If they don't remember, they will choose a date according to a number they like, a month that belongs to the season of the birth, and this will become the official birthday for all documents such as ID cards and passports. One of my "adoptive" daughters, a Tibetan, chose March 15 "because this is an important date for us Buddhists," she said.

According to the Chinese tradition, a child is said to be one year old on the first "Spring Festival" (New Year) following his birth, even if he was born one month before. And, also according to the tradition, each Chinese person adds a year of age on the seventh day of each new year of their life. This is why the Chinese ask a person's age saying: "*Jinnian duo da?*" meaning how old are you "this year"? A person is alleged to be the same age during the whole (Lunar) year.

Now we understand why the Chinese didn't used to celebrate birthdays, one by one, as we do, on the day a person was born, but on the 7th day of the lunar year – the day everyone change age. Only some anniversaries are important: 60 and 70. If you were in China one month before the 60th anniversary of the founding of New China, on October 1, 2009, you might have understood the importance of a 60th anniversary.

With the opening up of China, Westerners entered with their own traditions. Chinese were enthralled by the candles on the birthday cake and the colorful greeting cards. Mostly in universities where students learn a foreign language, the young Chinese started to celebrate their foreign teacher's birthday, offering a card as a gift, unsigned, and still wrapped it together with its envelope and the cellophane protector. If they had a little more money, or if they were a group, they would buy a cake and candles, and bring their "gift" to their teacher's apartment on the campus. This practice may be artless, but it is so imbued with deep respect and the desire to make someone happy, that I will never forget how many cakes and cards I got as gifts from Chinese students and friends.

Now it has become common for the Chinese to invite their friends to a restaurant for their birthday. Unlike in the West, the celebrated person pays the bill, while the guests bring some gifts.

For a newborn, the most important day is the 100th from his birth. On that day, the parents throw a big party in a restaurant for all their relatives, friends, and colleagues, and collect the red envelopes containing a gift of money for the baby.

The Chinese Lunar New Year (*Chunjie* or Spring Festival) is the best occasion to thank your Chinese friends to whom you owe something. They will more easily accept your gift and not consider it as payment for a service. But what should you offer? First, be sure to never offer a clock, as the Chinese are very keen on word associations, and *zhong* for clock is the homophone of the *zhong* meaning the end, as in *zhongdian* or terminal.

What to give to the Chinese? Liquor and cigarettes (personally I never poison my friends with tobacco) are appreciated by men, and you may notice that they are mostly offered in even numbers of cartons or bottles, a tradition that is compulsory only in the case of children offering them to their parents for the New Year. Now that people pay more attention to their health, they appreciate receiving ginseng or other products that they would not buy themselves. Fine chocolates, cookies, and dried fruit of high quality are also popular gifts. For children, the famous *hong bao*, red envelopes containing money, are always most appreciated.

People don't open a wrapped gift immediately and show their satisfaction? This is the way Chinese politeness goes. You normally open a gift privately, unless you are invited to do differently.

Yes-No, and He-She

Once I asked a Chinese colleague who visited my place, "Aren't you cold?" "Yes," he replied. So I shut the window, thinking he was feeling cold. I soon realized that he meant just the opposite as he was almost sweating. A negative-interrogative question such as "Aren't you cold?" is confusing for the Chinese counterpart. "Yes" means for the Chinese "he is not cold," or "I confirm that what you said in your question is right" as Chinese grammar goes. But for us who speak French, English, Italian, or Spanish, the natural answer would be "No (I'm not cold)."

Foreign friends who visit China often ask me why the Chinese say "yes" when they think "no." They reach the point where they think Chinese lie! The problem results from the way foreign languages are taught in China: by translation instead of using exclusively the taught language and creating circumstances that will suggest the appropriate responses. Thinking in our own mother tongue while speaking another language leads to funny misunderstandings.

Once I was on a train and a Chinese university lecturer told me a story about his sister and brother-in-law. In oral Chinese, the same pronoun *ta* covers both "he" and "she." As he used both pronouns indifferently in English, I was soon mixed up jumping from man to woman. I could only make out whom he was talking about through verbs such as "to be pregnant" or "to shave his beard."

Kissing strangers

I said formerly that the Chinese use the word "friend" often, as they call a person they have never met a friend. Then how is it that some Western women kiss their colleagues' husbands when they are introduced to each other?

The first time I had my Chinese students for a dinner at my place, on campus, I started to hug them when they left all together at 22:30. The first, then the second, who were close in proximity to me, had no chance to react as I embraced them spontaneously, taking them by surprise. But the others said in Chinese, "*Kuai, kuai zou* (Let's escape)," as they understood I was going to hug each one of them. I really regretted this, because I knew I should never kiss a Chinese person. In fact, I had forgotten the rule.

For the Chinese, physical contact is strictly reserved for lovers. Handshaking, a habit that entered China with the reform and opening up, is accepted, especially where non-Chinese are involved with Chinese, but this is not necessary. Two Chinese who meet for the first time exchange name cards and polite words, but usually don't shake hands. When they do, they often offer only their fingers or a limp hand, unaware that a firm handshake expresses sincerity and confidence. Some grasp your hand strongly and squeeze it as long as the conversation lasts. It's only because they have not learned this Western greeting.

Show off... the price

When a Chinese person invites you to a restaurant, he or she may tell you: "This fish is the most expensive on the menu." You may be shocked, as such words seem to be of a person who likes to show off his or her wealth. You would probably prefer to hear, "This is the best dish they prepare in this restaurant." In fact, the meaning is the same for Chinese, and their point when letting you know the price is to tell you how much they care for you, how precious your presence is among them, and how deep the respect is that they feel for you. You should then answer, "Thank you, I really don't deserve so much."

The whiter the better

For most Chinese people, especially women, we Caucasian Westerners are nice because our skin is white. Their cosmetics contain substances to keep the skin white or to make it whiter. They use umbrellas more often on sunny days than on rainy days. They invented a very elegant arm protector that they wear when they use their bicycles in summer, complete with gloves. On the beach, they spend most of the time under umbrellas. Some go to the sea with umbrellas or are even covered with towels. On the street you can see women who protect their faces from the sun holding magazines or even their purses high.

We must not be surprised by this. In old times, European women thought the same way: being dark implied that they were peasants working in the fields all day; it meant that they were people obliged to work to earn their life, while the nobles were closed in their palaces.

Today, more Chinese women enjoy holidays and they have money to travel; they go to the beach for a rest and are less frightened to get a suntan.

Sixty years ago, only a minority of the Chinese could eat their fill. People were generally skinny. In such a society, those who had a little fat were considered fortunate. Wasn't it the same in Italy, for instance? Today, obesity has become not only a new word in the language but a new social reality, especially among children, the "little emperors," who get their junk food when going back home after school and have no appetite for balanced meals. Adults, men as well as women, attend "get-fit classes" or exercise on their own to lose weight. There was a time when telling someone "You gained weight" was a compliment. Young people would avoid saying that nowadays. Only old people who suffered from hunger can still think this way. On the contrary, women are generally pleased to hear, "You've lost weight!"

Look at me when I talk to you!

Haven't you heard that when you were young? Maybe this is what you too say to your children or your students. Eyes are the mirror of the soul, says a proverb, and our Western culture considers that not looking the interlocutor in the eyes when talking indicates a lack of sincerity or even falseness.

In Chinese culture, eye contact is not only unnecessary but impolite. Looking directly to the person talking to you is like a challenge. Feelings and emotions should be kept private, and this has nothing to do with honesty or attention.

Making people walk out of malice?

Our Western practical mind can see only a lack of logic in a daily reality that consists into walking long distances between one and another bus line, or a bus stop and the subway station. Why doesn't the bus stop in front of the subway station instead of passing it and stopping 100 meters away?

If you come from a country like Canada, with a total

population equivalent to the one of the two cities of Beijing and Shanghai, it is perfectly natural that you react this way, and the Chinese way of thinking would be an act of pure spite in a city such as Montreal, Toronto, or Vancouver.

But in Beijing, when a hundred passengers get off the bus to transfer to the subway, when three or four bus lines stop concurrently at the same subway station, when hundreds and hundreds of commuters emerge from the subway station and run after one of these buses, could you imagine the mess if all of those persons would pack in and out at the same point? So, it is only logical to distribute them within a certain distance, as well as the only possible way to survive!

Chapter 3

We also act strangely in their eyes

In this chapter, I would like to introduce situations – thinking, doing, and saying – to be avoided in a Chinese environment.

Avoid "to steal"

Once, a young American man came to visit China. He was recommended by my friends, so I took care of him. When he traveled south, I arranged his stay with a Chinese family, who hosted him with all the due respect to a "guest from afar." He enjoyed his own bedroom and his meals for free.

One day, while the family was watching TV, he came out of his room and started searching the living-room, moving the sofa cushions, and looking under the furniture and behind the TV set. As he failed to find his wallet, he said, in his bad Chinese, "Someone must have taken it!" looking directly into the eyes of the three people of the family, one by one. "I had 800 Yuan in it," he added. The couple was so embarrassed that the man immediately phoned me, in Beijing, asking me to explain in English to the "visitor from afar" that he was committing the biggest mistake ever and then he told me he would offer the young man the lost amount the next day, as soon as the bank opened. Years have passed, and the Chinese family forgot the boy's name but still remember the unbearable offence.

If ever you lose anything in one's house, first, search discreetly, not in front of them. Avoid putting them in a situation where they could feel suspect. This is basic and compulsory. The habit of taking on the guilt on one's self is so deeply rooted in Chinese culture that even when you go to a police station to make a declaration, after your passport and money have been obviously robbed on a bus, the words used verbally by the police as well as in the written report are "lost" and "to lose," not "robbed" or "to steal."

Don't climb the stairs four by four

It is tedious for Westerners who are used to efficiency and quickness (well, not in all countries...) to follow the Chinese hierarchy when it comes to ask for permission or a service. For example, let's say you rent an apartment and water leaks in from the floor above you. To whom will you complain? Not to the service workers, even if there is one passing your door when you open it, or to the company in charge of maintenance, which has its office on the first floor, but to the apartment's owner. He is away on a business trip? What a pity, you will have to wait. If you proceed differently, the workers will not forward your complaint, and the caretaker company will not answer you but communicate with the owner anyway, if they do anything.

There are always several levels to the process, and you will gain nothing by trying to run faster than the train and going directly to the top. Remember the chair story I told you in "Basic Secrets" at the beginning.

Avoid bargaining if you have not made your decision

This is one of the most important and common mistakes foreigners make in China. In Asian countries, bargaining is part of the game when it comes to selling-buying. Prices are fixed very high, extremely high in markets that mostly foreigners frequent, as a way to leave margin for the game. For example, the price of a *pashmina* scarf is written as 300 Yuan, right before my eyes. But when I ask, "*Ni mai duoshao qian?*" ("What's your price?"), the answer is never more than

one-third of the marked price, and they add, "For you, old friend." If you are a newcomer (which is easy to detect, even if you speak Chinese), you may be called "old friend" equally, but your price will be 200 Yuan. Vendors know that long-time residents are aware of the market, including merchandise and prices, and it's useless for them to start the game too high.

It's correct to ask for the price. But don't continue to the next step if you have not decided to buy! The next step would be "*Pianyi yidian'r?*" ("Cheaper?"); it's the beginning of the bargaining game. Vendors answer this question with another question: "How much do you want to pay?" Let's take a real situation. I was passing a stall of linen scarves, new models on the market, and the vendor said, "120." As I continued to walk on, she added immediately, "80 for you!" I said, "I would give you 20, is that okay?" certain that she would leave me alone. And I went looking at other merchandise at the next stall. She pursued the game by herself: "85! 70! 65-last-price!" I didn't pay any attention to her and definitively moved away. It was her last chance to say, "Okay, okay, 20!" I was done. I had to buy it as I announced that amount myself and she lowered her price to meet my offer. Fortunately, though I didn't need the scarf, I really love it and still wear it after six years.

When you are asked how much you want to pay, don't say any price if you have not decided to buy, and don't say the real price you would pay if you want to buy, but lower than that. You must save some room for bargaining. The vendor will come down little by little and ask you, as it's normal in such a game, to "add a little more" to the point where you both will meet in the middle. So you must give yourself a chance to go up and up to the price you think is right for you. Anyway, you will always win at the end. If ever the vendor lets you go, after long negotiations, without recalling you, it means your price was really exaggerated.

I would say half the foreigners quit the game before the end. Moreover, they say, "I'll come back." The Chinese make fun of us for this expression, to the point that if you don't say it, they will tease you, "Maybe you come back, yes?"

Almost everything may be bargained for in China. Some foreigners who are not used to bargaining prefer to buy in supermarkets, where the prices are fixed. It's half a solution. When it comes to fresh fruit and vegetables, the prices are much higher than they are in public markets, the merchandise is not as fresh, and you can't choose it as it is already wrapped. In large, covered markets, you will seldom be cheated. Prices are fixed daily by the State on fruit, vegetable, meat, eggs, cereals, etc. There is no need to bargain; if you do it, it will be without big results.

Bargaining is my favorite activity. I never go shopping with Chinese when it's for me, as they are too shy to bargain, or they accept – instead of me – a discounted price still much higher than what I want to pay and which I know I can obtain. Once they have said, "Okay," the game is finished and I can't continue bargaining. But, on the other hand, my Chinese friends often ask me to accompany them shopping. Here is a story. At my last work position, a colleague bought a blouse in a nearby department store*, and she showed it to me: "Guess how much I paid?" I said, "80." "How do you know?" she asked, staring at me, wide-eyed. "Because I know you," I said, "and because I saw this blouse at 120 Yuan, and I think you would estimate one-third less." After a while I dared add, "But... I must tell you I bought the same for 25 Yuan last week."

Another story goes: I accompanied two foreign friends to Xi'an. They didn't speak any Chinese. After visiting the Terracotta Army Pits, we wanted to buy some souvenirs to bring home and chose a set of three soldiers and one horse. We bought 28 boxes altogether. When we went back to the car we had rented, the driver exclaimed, "Why didn't you call me to bargain for you? You are foreigners, you surely paid too much!" I told him the starting price was 35 a set and asked how much he could have paid. Without hesitation, he said, "15, maximum 18." "Then I had a good deal, as we paid 7.5 Yuan a box."

---

* Each counter is independent. Private merchants rent a space and do their own business.

Don't plant bamboo in a rice field

Incense sticks are planted three by three in a sand base, inside or in front of a temple. A pair of chopsticks are planted vertically in a bowl of rice only beside the bed of a dead person. It doesn't take a long story to explain that one should never plant chopsticks in the rice at table. They can be placed horizontally on the special holder or on the individual plate or bowl. Don't keep them in your hands when you are not using them.

Don't trust a Chinese smile

Several foreigners measure their own behavior on the smile of their Chinese counterpart. Often, when I tell Western friends visiting China that they should not say this or do that, they answer, "I have, and the Chinese were very happy with it!"

When a Chinese person smiles, it doesn't mean he or she is happy. It's far from meaning you have done well. Chinese politeness requires never showing negative feelings, like those that a person's behavior could have instigated, let apart expressing reproaches to someone.

A Chinese person smiles when he or she is embarrassed or even deeply offended. For sure, contentment, satisfaction, happiness are also expressed through smiles. It will take you some time to notice the difference between the two opposite kinds of smiles. I must insist: don't measure your social aptitude in Chinese life by the smiles you see around you.

If at some point you suspect you have done something wrong according to the Chinese culture or tradition, and you want a true answer, don't check with the presumed offended person. Telling you the truth would be equivalent to reproaching you, so this person would necessarily hide the truth. You should ask another Chinese person not involved in the situation, without mentioning that "you" were the person in question. Just pretend a fake, neutral situation.

In all circumstances, remember that, in Chinese culture, what is unsaid is much more important that what is spoken.

Don't say don't

Try to avoid rough verbs such as *yao and bu yao* (I want, I don't want). Replace them with the sweet expression "*Wo xiang yao...*" or "*Wo xiang mai...*," meaning "I would like," "I think I will buy this one."

To the question "Would you like some beer?" don't answer "*Bu yao*" but "*Bu xiang yao*" or "*Bu xiang he*" ("I don't think I will have any/drink," or "*Bu xiguan*" ("I'm not used to it")" instead of "*Bu xihuan*" ("I don't like").

Don't touch private parts

In some Western cultures, women especially, on seeing a baby, like to touch its face, pinch its cheeks, even take it in their arms and kiss it all over. But this kind of enthusiasm is not welcomed in Chinese culture.

Affection is a private feeling and is kept for family members. Mostly, it's impolite to caress or touch the head of a child.

And if you want to give a candy to a child on the street or in a park, ask the father or the grandmother (children are never alone!) if you can, first. They will say no, out of politeness, and if you want to insist, give the candy to them instead of to the child directly.

Look in the mirror before criticizing

One of the things most non-Chinese can't stand about the Chinese is that they spit in public and everywhere. After two decades here I'm still unable to close my eyes on this bad habit. I have commented enough in my books and articles and I will not repeat my comments here. We also dislike their habit of clearing their throats noisily. And we find that they speak and laugh loudly as if they were alone in a bus, a restaurant, or on a street. All this is true, and unbearable for us.

But have we ever thought there were points that they

can't stand about us? Let's see some basic ones. If ever you have seen foreigners taking a handkerchief from their pocket or handbag, blow their nose loudly (or even quietly,) among the people they were talking with, and put the handkerchief (or worse: a paper tissue) back in their pocket, you might have noticed how embarrassed the Chinese were seeing that. They might have tried to continue the conversation as if nothing strange had happened, but the display to which they were exposed was too disgusting to ever be forgotten. A Chinese person in the same situation would apologize and leave the room. If someone is talking at that moment, in order to not interrupt, he would rather sniffle than blow his nose publicly. I know, sniffling is not approved of in Western society, and a Westerner who sneezes in public will apologize, while a Chinese person finds this natural as we have no control on sudden sneezing. Strange? This is the way things are.

Don't fall into the trap

This is my last point but not the least. There is a cultural habit that may become a trap to foreigners. The Chinese used to praise "the guest from afar" as a light on their life. When they welcome foreign experts who come to work in China, they invite them to "criticize" China, or their work, or their daily life, and to use their wisdom to give them advice that will help the people and the country to improve. This is a polite way to welcome a foreigner and to show respect.

But most foreigners don't pass the test and fall

into the trap, though the situation doesn't aim to trap or test on the part of the Chinese. When a Chinese person invites a foreigner to comment and show them what is wrong in China, this person is not expecting a positive reply but a humble one such as "China has such an old culture, how could our country with less than a millennium of existence (for the United States or Canada, for example) teach China what to do?" I know you feel bad talking this way, while after a few days in this country you already have a long list of recriminations against China, but if you say something like, "Yes, I noticed that you Chinese do this and that, but you should do that and this," you're done! Be humble, shut your mouth, and wait for the Chinese to insist, two or three months later, before daring to teach them a behavior or social manners that you think are "the" best. Maybe by that time will you have observed, compared, understood, and decided that 'after all, it was not so bad.'

In the same spirit, avoid giving advice to other people's children. Once, in Kunming, I was shopping with a friend and her daughter. The little girl ate candies and scattered papers all along our way. I knew it was not my role to educate the child, but I couldn't stand such a behavior and wanted the mother to know what I thought. So, I gathered the papers one after the other and kept them in my hand until I found a garbage can. The mother knew I did it on purpose and she remained silent. It was not nice of me to do so, but I played up the fact that I was new in China, and my friend would think I was unaware of the rules of Chinese politeness.

Another thing that the Chinese will never tell you that they hate is when a person gossips about the wrongdoings of another, especially if the third person is known by the one to whom you are talking. If you publicly expose the lack of *savoir-vivre* or the mistakes of an absent party, your interlocutor will immediately imagine that you tell others what he or she does, too. You may ask yourself why I write this here, as in our Western culture, especially the Christian culture, one should refrain from speaking ill of others. But this is not what we always do...

Several non-Chinese have asked me why the Chinese don't talk about themselves or their families. Personal life is considered a matter that is not worth exposing to others. It doesn't result in anything good or improve others' lives to know that your wife had a surgery last week or that your son is saving pocket money to buy a great bicycle at the end of the year.

There is another reason for the silence. According to Confucius' teachings, one should not express feelings, especially negative ones that could only add burden on a friend's shoulder and sadden the heart. What about the positive feelings, such as the pride of a mother whose daughter won first prize in a piano competition or whose son had been chosen to go abroad practicing his English during the summer holidays? Unless asked about his or her children (or other aspects of life), a Chinese person will keep the news close, in order not to be seen as one who wants to show off or make others jealous.

Chapter 4

How do the Chinese see us?

Well, this is not an easy topic to discuss. Generally speaking, the Chinese vision of Westerners is ambivalent. On the one hand, they find us rude and boastful, but don't show or say it. We also find them rude with each other and with persons they consider inferior to them such as a restaurant waitress or a manual worker, anyone whose function is "serving." On the other hand, the Chinese admire the Westerners whose countries have reached a high scientific and technological level, wealth, and comfortable living conditions.

Why are we "rude" in their eyes? Because we are too direct in saying what we think and in the way we think. What is a revered quality for us is an offence to them. What would be hypocrisy for us is respect and politeness for them. We also treat our business partners like possible opponents, ready to challenge us, and we believe only in documents that could become weapons in court if ever we are cheated.

Let's take the example of a contract between Chinese and non-Chinese. For a Westerner, whatever is not included in a contract doesn't exist, and all that is written and signed is immutable and obligatory.

When I started working in China, foreign experts had no written contract but a verbal one. The university had promised to give me a teaching position, with housing facilities, and retain me for one year, and I had promised to do my job the best I could and to stay till the end of the year. Several foreigners working in China used the fact that they didn't sign any contract as an opportunity to escape their commitments when they didn't like their jobs. Some quit the country secretly and never came back, leaving three or four classes without a teacher for several weeks, sometimes. The situation was so common that a monetary guarantee was later imposed on foreign workers from the moment they took their positions, and the salary was paid at the end of the month for newcomers instead of at the beginning as it was for us, the established ones.

The traditional Chinese way of negotiation and contract consisted in a series of steps: knowing, understanding, and appreciating mutually. At first, both parties would have tea together; a second or third meeting would be about testing the partner's honesty and capacities, and making friends. Then, the partners would sign a letter of intention and, later, a letter of agreement. A contract meant "we know and respect each other enough to be willing to accomplish something together. We trust each other and believe we can sit together and find solutions to eventual problems." Contracts didn't specify details, deadlines, costs, and responsibilities. Both partners were morally committed to do their best to bring their project to an end.

Nowadays, the Chinese know the Western way and accommodate it, but, deep in their minds, they

EVERGREEN GALLERY

名筑画廊

Dear Lisa.

Our gallery will hold exhibition for you on January 7 1995.

Now. we send the name card of frame word Corp. you can contact with them.

1994 Nov. 27.

still consider a verbal engagement to be more important than a signature on a piece of paper.

In 1995, I had a painting exhibition in a Beijing gallery. As I was a Westerner, the gallery owner asked his assistant to prepare a contract for me. I had not asked for it, as I was already used to the Chinese way, and I knew what they said they would do would certainly be done. The "contract" consisted of two sentences, and when I saw it, I hardly refrained from laughing.

The word "Dear" that also appears in e-mails written to strangers come from the West and is used when Chinese address foreigners.

Though Westerners are not completely admirable on the whole, the Chinese have a desire to imitate us and to adopt our lifestyles. In a sense, they consider developed countries as superior. Imitation doesn't always produce happy results. Let's take the wedding example. As the Chinese don't know the meaning of the white wedding gown, we can see widows who remarry, or a bride who marries in her 50s, in a white dress. Because it was pretty, the Western-style wedding dress had been a fashion, at a certain time, for singers, performance MCs. As for weddings, the model was kept but the color changed. The Chinese use the diamond ring we usually use for engagement as a wedding band, and they often wear it in the middle finger of right or left hand.

The Chinese also adopt and adapt foreign culture to theirs. When they translate a text about Chinese culture into a Western language, they write, for example, "June 15 of the lunar calendar." First of all, several lunar calendars are used in the world and they don't all start on the same Moon. They should more precisely say "the Chinese lunar calendar." The second mistake is that April, May, June, etc. belong to the Gregorian calendar, which is presently used in the West, while the Chinese use numbers for their months. When they say June, they mean the 6th month, which, in fact, starts around mid-July according to the Gregorian calendar.

Once I went to visit a friend, but never found her at the address she had given me. I knocked on all the doors on the 4th floor, but no one knew her. In fact, her apartment was on the 5th floor, but because she was talking to a Westerner, she added one as some – though not all – countries do. But as I had got the address from a Chinese, I had considered that ground floor was the first.

Another day, a Chinese computer technician gave me his name card. As he expected customers in the foreign community, he had his name printed Jin Gao. I called three times and asked for Mr. Jin, but never found him. His family name was Gao, and he had reversed the order the Western way.

In textbooks designated to foreigners who learn the Chinese language, the "Hello" greeting is "*Ni hao ma?*" This is what we all learned, isn't it? But "*ni hao ma*" is a question, the exact translation of "How do you do?" that was used in the United States before. The Chinese adapted their own culture to the Americans! They usually say *Ni hao*, word for word "you good," or "I wish you good."

The 7th day of the 7th Chinese lunar month is the Qixi festival, unknown outside China and not even very popular in China. Five or six years ago, the Chinese media started to publicize the *Qixi* calling it "Chinese Valentine's Day," a big mistake in my eyes. Instead of promoting Chinese culture, the "Chinese Lovers' Day" became a mere copy of one more Western festival.

Once, I had a silver "13" on a chain around my neck. Several Chinese told me, that day, "Why do you wear this? It's an unlucky number!" In the Friendship Hotel where I had been living for 11 years, there was no apartment 13, because the buildings were reserved for foreigners. For example, the 5th floor had numbers 511, 512, 514, 515.

In several hotel elevators or elevators in buildings where non-Chinese live, we may find floors 12a, 12b, 14, but no 13. As number 4, the homophone of "death," is the unlucky number for the Chinese, some elevators have no 4, 13, 14, 24, 34. So the 35-story building has, in fact, 30 floors.

Legends about the origin of the unlucky 13 are too numerous to recount here. Most are related to Christianity, to Nordic mythology, or to October 13, 1307, in France.

There is another point I would like to mention. When I was with CCTV, my Canadian colleague sitting with me on the backseat of the car tapped the shoulder of the Chinese woman on the front seat, because he wanted to say goodbye when getting off and didn't know her name. She never forgot "the arrogant and uncivilized man who dared touch me." Such a reaction was perfectly normal for a Chinese person. Starting around the beginning of the new century, in markets highly visited by foreigners, vendors, mostly girls, touch the customers to be friendly. Once, I accompanied a 30-ish visitor from Canada to the

Silk Market. The vendor put her hand on his shoulder while coaxing him with her "good-price-for-you-my-friend." He was embarrassed but didn't dare say anything to the intruder. He asked me, in French, whether this was a Chinese custom. "Absolutely not!" I said, and I asked the girl to keep her hands to herself. She laughed sarcastically and even dared say I was jealous! "You Westerners do this way," she thought. I explained that some may not mind, but not all of us like to be touched by strangers.

In conclusion to the question "How do the Chinese see us," I must say something unpleasant but important. It seems to me that the Chinese are afraid to assert themselves, to be different from their peers, and to be criticized. We can notice that in their classrooms where no student dares to oppose the teacher with his or her own opinion or offer a different view from the rest of the class. And they don't change this once they enter the work market. Adults among them do the same with their bosses and colleagues in a meeting: standard thought, standard talk. But there is more: When they talk with a foreigner who enquires about their country, politics, culture, society, some answer the official way (what should be said, not what they think), and some say what the foreigner likes to hear. If there is no witness around, they may even speak against China and its government to show you they are "open-minded." Recently, workers at my home asked me why I like China, adding that "Chinese people have no human rights." When I asked them which right they missed, the three of them were unable to go further except for saying, "You foreigners all say that." So, be aware! This happens more often than you may think.

I have heard Chinese forwarding old stereotypes (such as China is a materialistic, totalitarian and repressive country) when telling stories that happened to them, or because they didn't get the real interpretation of facts, or because it was more convenient to them than trying to explain a complex reality.

Sometimes misunderstandings are due to the fact that both speakers or one of them are speaking in a foreign language, English or Chinese in most cases. Once I was talking in Chinese with a Tibetan friend and his cousin, a Lama monk. I asked them whether they were aware that a large part of the Western world think that Tibetans are deprived of religious freedom. Nodding, they said, "*Dui, meiyou ziyou.* ("Right, we have no freedom.") As I know there is freedom, I was astonished and wanted to understand where our conversation lacked clarity. I asked in detail, "Do you have to hide to go to the temple? Would a Tibetan be arrested if he prays publicly, turns the prayer mills openly, or adds a stone or scented herbs to the heap? Is a Tibetan forbidden to go on a pilgrimage, or to take part in religious ceremonies?" To each of my questions, the answer was obviously, "No." They even smiled at my "candid" questions and asked me why I had doubts. I countered, "Why do you say you don't enjoy religious freedom, then?" "We have no choice of religion," they said again. "Tibetans are born Lamaists (Tibetan Buddhists). We are all Lamaists." And I imagined the pleasure of a foreign journalist, eager to quote "Tibetan victims of the Chinese policies," hearing them...

Chapter 5

It was a good time after all...

Under the influence of the opening-up policy of China and the impact of its exchanges with the outside world, all aspects of life in this country have changed tremendously. Let's glance at some of these changes through my personal experience in the last two decades.

In 1991, I was hired as a French and Italian teacher in a Beijing university. In the teachers' building, in winter, we had heating and hot water two hours in the morning and four hours in the evening. Every unit in the city had water and power cut one day per week, in turn, to allow for better service to all. There was no heating in the classroom building, and students had to keep their gloves, scarves, and hats on during the lessons. But the following year, a new building was ready, which was overheated, with sealed windows... and they all fell asleep in the class. There was no heating in stores, buses, cinemas, etc.

Public buses didn't run after 21:00 and several lines not after 20:00. This is why evening shows were scheduled at 18:00 or 18:30 and lasted only one hour. Chinese were used to dining at 17:30 and all was done by 18:00.

Restaurants closed at 20:00. At 6:40 every day, there were compulsory physical exercises on the campus, and free *taiji* classes for teachers. Each work

unit had its own morning exercises. There was nothing to do in the evenings, so Chinese people used to go to bed early and get up early. Breakfast could be bought on the street for the family. Only elderly, ill people, and children were allowed to buy milk (production was not sufficient at that time) and a family member had to line up every morning to get about 300 ml.

Products like cereals, oil, and sugar were still

rationed, and tickets were needed to buy them. Unregistered residents of Beijing, including foreigners, obviously, could not have ration tickets, except on the black market or, in my case, tickets given by students.

There was a "Change Money" black market where foreigners could get Chinese Yuan for their dollars instead of Foreign Exchange Certificates. The FECs were guaranteed and official, but they could be used only in stores that were authorized by the State to sell to foreigners. Abacuses prevailed in stores, and users were astonishingly fast.

Hygiene conditions were far from adequate. Hospitals said they used "*yi ci yong*" (single use) syringes, but what they meant was that they would wash them (in cold water and without soap) after use. Public toilets were as rare as hair on a bald head. Most of the time they had no water to flush, no water to wash hands, and, of course, no soap.

Goods like wine, fruit juice, coffee, cheese, and olives could not be purchased in China. Good Chinese products such as ice cream and toothpaste were quickly purchased or merged with foreign companies. After-sale service was an unknown reality. Lettuce, round cabbage, broccoli, and snow peas had not yet penetrated the Chinese market.

Traveling, even within China, was only a dream for the Chinese, let alone going abroad. Holidays served to go back to their native places to spend festivals with families. Airplanes served to go only abroad; national airlines were too expensive for the local population. Even the subway was too expensive. The bicycle was "the" mode of transportation: for moving, buying a TV, or carrying to the hospital a woman who was about to give birth.

Foreigners were seen as wealthy, no matter where they came from. Those who, like myself, were working in a State unit for 1/20th of their salary at home were still earning three times more than a local Chinese person. Admission to museums, historical or cultural sites was ten times higher for foreigners than locals. For instance, it cost 3 Yuan for foreigners to enter the Forbidden City, but only 0.3 Yuan for Chinese citizens. However, "foreign experts" working for a State unit in China enjoyed the privilege of a white card (later yellow, and finally orange) allowing them to pay an intermediate price for these admissions as well as for train tickets, excluding flights. A 7-Yuan book was considered a very

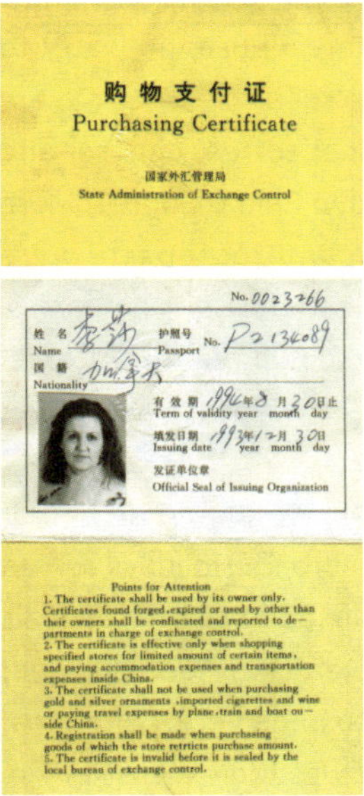
购物支付证
Purchasing Certificate

国家外汇管理局
State Administration of Exchange Control

No. 0023266

姓名 Name
护照号 Passport No. P2134089
国籍 Nationality
有效期 1994年8月30日止 Term of validity year month day
填发日期 1993年12月30日 Issuing date year month day
发证单位章 Official Seal of Issuing Organization

Points for Attention
1. The certificate shall be used by its owner only. Certificates found forged, expired or used by other than their owners shall be confiscated and reported to departments in charge of exchange control.
2. The certificate is effective only when shopping specified stores for limited amount of certain items, and paying accommodation expenses and transportation expenses inside China.
3. The certificate shall not be used when purchasing gold and silver ornaments, imported cigarettes and wine or paying travel expenses by plane, train and boat outside China.
4. Registration shall be made when purchasing goods of which the store retrticts purchase amount.
5. The certificate is invalid before it is sealed by the local bureau of exchange control.

expensive book. The third floor of a certain bookstore sold pirated books. There, a Webster English-Chinese complete dictionary sold for 6 Yuan, but no foreigner was allowed to set foot on the illegal 3rd floor.

At that time, housing was provided by each danwei or work unit. A commercial housing market was non-existent. Foreigners could not rent or buy an apartment. Tourists stayed in hotels, and foreign experts were housed by their unit. But we were not free... The campus gate closed at 21:00. If one was late, the only way in was to climb over the 3-meter gate. The guards could see you but would not open the gate.

"*Danwei*" is a very interesting word (and reality) that I would like to explain here. Though it has almost disappeared, it was the "little world" to which each Chinese belonged.

The *danwei* was responsible for every aspect of life: from birth to funeral, from marriage to giving birth and schooling children; from providing housing to health services, cultural life, entertainment, etc. Films were shown every Friday evening; public showers, cafeteria, public telephone and post office, clinic, bank – all were on its grounds. Morning exercises were set by the *danwei*; control of private lives also belonged to the *danwei*. Permission for divorce had to be obtained from it. A *danwei* had its own cars with drivers. "My *danwei*, your *danwei* were words one would hear several times a day. A little boy said once, "My father works as a driver, my mother as a teacher; so who in our family works for the *danwei*?"

Foreigners working for the international radio or

in the publishing field were housed at the Friendship Hotel. When a Chinese visited a foreigner, he had to sign upon arriving and leaving, and the foreigners had to go and meet the guest at the gate. At 20:00, a phone call reminded the foreigner that the time had come for the guest to leave. Only certified married couples could live together, even when both were foreigners. Don't even think about a Chinese person spending a night with a foreigner...

Foreigners' mail was inspected, especially the first and the last two months of the contract. Envelopes were often delivered with the glue still wet, and photos were often missing. Once I got a page in German in my daughter's letter; this page belonged to my German neighbor...

The elegant Chinese wore long underpants visible through their nylons. Young beauties wore mini-skirts with knee-high stockings and socks with their sandals. Through the side slit of a *qipao* (Chinese dress) one could see the stocking's elastic top. Sundresses were first seen after 1995, and were worn over a T-shirt. Men proudly exposed the brand of their Western suit on the sleeve.

Today the Chinese move around the country and non-Chinese are so numerous that even the rural Chinese have seen at least one foreigner face to face. But 20 years ago, parents with their child in a park on a summer day would timidly ask a foreign passerby to have his or her picture taken with their child, then with themselves. "The" dream of all Chinese was to go abroad for a visit. They also thought that every non-

Chinese person in the world was rich, had a house with a garden, servants and maids, at least one car, and was Christian.

Well, it was a good time... I came to China at the right moment to see the rapid evolution from the past to the future. Some images will always remain printed in my mind: Chinese used to squat while they waited for a bus; there was no advertising on television; newspapers could be read exclusively on *baolan* (boards) installed along the streets...

There is one thing: most Chinese of the post-1980 generation don't know their own culture. They don't know what is new, what is old; they ignore what is Chinese and what comes from abroad. For example, if you tell a young Chinese, "Your English is very good!" he will answer "Thank you!" This is nothing bad. But if you delve deeper into conversation, you will discover that he doesn't know that his parents' generation would have refused the compliment by saying, "You are flattering me!" or "You exaggerate, I speak very little English."

A very special image

There are some interesting Chinese inventions that I would like to mention here before they disappear or because I find them very ingenious. In winter, men from the countryside used to wear a hand-knitted strip protecting their ears and chin from the cold. This "piece of clothing" was placed on top of the ears, just like the plastic covers the hairdressers use when dyeing hair, and crossing under the chin.

Another example of the Chinese ingenuity resides in the babies' and toddlers' pants with a hole at the place we would cover first. This is to facilitate the answer to the call of nature and avoid having to change the child after each accident. It is surely efficient as Chinese children are clean much earlier than our children.

Women mostly wear a sleeve protector that covers the clothes from wrist to elbow and that is easier to wash than the whole clothes. It's not typically Chinese, as we use to wear that when I was a pupil in primary school where we had white collar and wrists on our black dress, but it is still used in China while it has vanished in the rest in the world.

As we know, the Chinese women like to keep their skin as white as possible. Avoiding sunshine is one of their most important concerns. When riding a bicycle,

they wear gloves or a pair of long sleeves with an elastic ring for the middle finger to keep their hands also well covered. Another neck-shoulder-arm-hand protector is made by a kind of collar with two long sleeves hooked to

the middle finger. No need to add that they also wear a large brim hat and sunglasses. When they go out on foot, they never forget to open their umbrellas, and, in case they have no umbrella, they hold their purses, their grocery bags, or a newspaper between the sun and their faces.

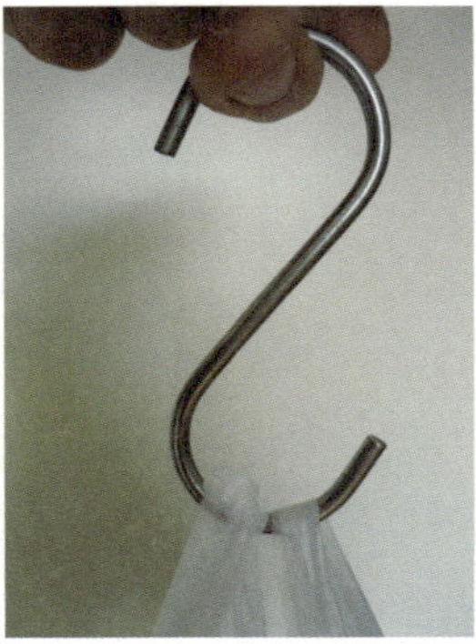

When buying beer or water bottles, instead of putting them in a bag, they tie the tops together with a string for easy carrying. On public buses, we often see elderly hanging their heavy bags to the horizontal hand pole with an aluminum S-shaped hook, which they always carry in their pockets.

In restaurants, when you put your jacket on the back of your chair, a waitress immediately covers it with a kind of pillow case that helps prevent grease or liquids from spilling on it during service and also keeps unwanted hands from freeing the jacket's contents. Restaurants also provide thin plastic gloves when customers order pig feet, crab, or anything that must be eaten with the hands.

Chapter 6

Is there anything wrong?

More often than not, I have been labeled "unconditional pro-China." This is not right. I love China deeply because it's the country I have been living in more happily than anywhere else in my life. However, my vision is aware of its gaps as well as its marvels. When I write for the Chinese, I criticize their behavior when I have to. This booklet is for the non-Chinese and aims to explain misconceptions that lead to annoyance, uneasiness, and even hatred, not to defend the Chinese and not to prove the superiority of one culture over another.

Translation mania

Although I feel comfortable and happy in China, there are two things that I can barely stand. The first is the mania of translating everything. A Chinese friend, a translator from Chinese to French, called me once to ask the meaning of "kiss" in Chinese. "In which context?" I asked. "It's the name of a band." "Oh! Then it should remain Kiss in your French text." But they always pretend that the readers will not get the "meaning." And this is how Hard Rock music became "a hard stone" in Chinese, and Charlie Chaplin, Cha-li Zhuo-bie-lin.

Names like Napoli and Venezia have been translated not from Italian but from English: Nabulesi (Naples) and Weinisi (Venice). The Italian name Francesco becomes Francisco as in Spanish in translation – fu-lang-xi-si-ke, without consideration for the culture or the context represented. "Canada" and "Canon" could easily be translated Ka-na-da and Ka-nong, but the characters for *ka* "are not nice to see," say the Chinese, so these names became *Jianada* and *Jianeng*, with two different characters for *jia* (respectively "to add" and "nice").

When I visit an exhibition, I don't even recognize the names of the Western artists after they have been translated. Why not write the names in the original language, and, in parentheses if necessary, the Chinese characters that would indicate the closest pronunciation, whether or not they are nice.

Tendency to generalization

The second thing that really disturbs me in the Chinese mentality is the tendency to generalize. Even if you don't know Chinese language, just listen to a conversation between two Chinese on the street, in a café (which is often translated into "Coffee") or in the subway. I'm sure you will catch the words "*guowai*" and "*guonei*" several times. Out of the country and in the country is the way the Chinese divide the world. This mentality is so rooted in their minds that even in Toronto, they call the other Canadian nationals "*waiguoren*" (foreigners).

"Do you foreigners eat mutton meat?," "Foreign

women like to wear blue," "Foreigners send their children live by themselves when they reach 18," "German people go to bed at 21:00," "Americans exchange their wives with their friends," and all kinds of allegations are based on one example, one single case, or one movie. When I am confronted with such a situation, I ask the Chinese counterpart whether northern China and southern China people all eat *jiaozi* on New Year's Eve, and they realize that, in the south, they have noodles, *tangyuan*, etc., instead of *jiaozi*. I ask whether a Muslim wedding proceeds the same way as a Han wedding. Are the Miao ethnic children educated the same way as the Uyghur? They finally admit that each region, sex, age, cultural background, religion, and family history must be considered differently and that each person, in fact, is unique! But why is it so difficult to change this mentality?

Economic globalization automatically dragged the world into cultural globalization. And globalization is American. Chinese know a little about American culture, and this is what they call foreign culture. For instance, they generally have the impression that all other countries celebrate Christmas on December 25 including the Russian Orthodox (Jan. 7), that all countries decorate a Christmas tree and

dine on roasted turkey. They never heard that Santa Claus we know today, plump and jolly, was created by Haddon Sundblom on the base of the Dutch Sinterklaas, a bishop, an image brought by settlers to New York in the 17th century, and that Coca-Cola, in 1931, capitalized on the figure for marketing purposes. But he belongs to the American culture, while Italians, for example, have the *Befana*. They stick Santa Claus posters on their neighbors' doors if they are foreigners, and wish Merry Xmas to Muslims as well as to Christians indiscriminately.

Two Canadians were hired to teach English in a Nanjing institute. On Dec. 24, they got an invitation for the same evening. When they entered the hall, there was music, balloons, a Christmas tree, and a buffet. The two of them were not Christian and had never celebrated Christmas before. All the other foreign experts were Japanese and Korean, and they didn't know what the theme of the party was.

On December 31, at midnight, Italians throw out the old year through the windows with old furniture, clothes, newspapers, all the old things they have collected for the occasion in the last weeks of the year. In Spain, on the twelfth ring of midnight, each person swallows a grape for happiness for each month of the new year.

Popular beliefs belong to each nation. We non-Chinese don't know them all, certainly, but, often when we hear a story, we ask where, when, who. I think that – generally speaking – we are open to the diversity of the world and don't take the singular for the regular, though we like to joke about blondes, "newfies," and "frogs."

Here are some examples of traditions related to weddings. In North America, people usually marry on Saturday and, in Italy, on Sunday. For Italian people, *ne di Marte ne di Venere* (never on Tuesday or Friday) when it comes to marry or to travel, but Wednesday brings good luck and Monday, money. According to a British tradition, the bride should wear something new, something old, something borrowed, and something blue. In Russian churches, before the bride and groom is a small silk carpet. The person who first puts a foot on it will command the household. So, both manage to put their feet together on the carpet. At the wedding banquet, Italian people use their forks and knives to clink on the glasses till the *sposini* (newlyweds) finally decide to kiss each other and put an end to the noise. In a Russian wedding party, the guests shout "Gor'ko" (bitter), and the newlyweds kiss

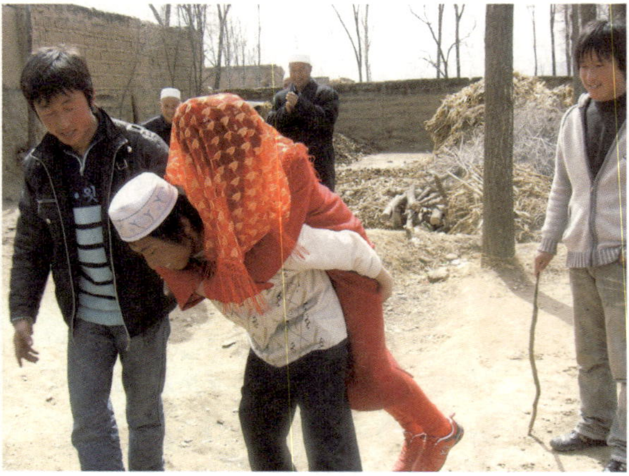

publicly to show that their love is not bitter, but sweet. The Muslim Hui groom in China's Ningxia Autonomous Region carries his wife on his back as a promise of supporting her in the difficulties of life. In the United States, at the end of the wedding party, the bride, turning her back to the unmarried female guests, throws her bouquet into the air. The one who catches it is supposed to get married next.

Chapter 7

Is integration a kind of cultural prostitution?

Integration is not assimilation. *Waiguoren* (literally "people from outside the country") often react negatively to my proposal. Integrating the Chinese society doesn't mean abandoning your own culture and becoming Chinese. It doesn't mean condemning all that is Western and elevating all that is Chinese. It is not changing what we are into others. But it is making ourselves feel at ease among the Chinese. This requires observation, reflection, and adaptation. It means finding our own place in Chinese society and making space for ourselves.

I don't know why, but the Chinese are more culture-conscious than we Westerners are. They always explain their traditions, they always tell us the why, when, and how of their customs, while we generally "live" our traditions without questioning. So, when we are out of our own country, it happens that the host country people – the Chinese in the present situation – ask us questions that we are not ready to answer. For instance, it's only when a Chinese person asked me where "Santa Claus" came from that I started to research about the figure.

On the other hand, the Chinese have a deeply rooted

tendency to generalize, as we said before. As the United States culture is the one they know best – though they know it superficially and often wrongly, but still more than we generally know Asian culture and Chinese culture in the present case – they think that Xmas is the "Western New Year," that it is celebrated by all non-Chinese, and that we all eat roasted turkey on that day, etc. No matter if you are an Orthodox Russian, they will wish you Merry Xmas on Dec. 25 (and till mid-January,) and "you" here includes the Buddhist Japanese or Thai as well as the Muslim Arabic nations.

Here we have a role to play: cultural education. I don't lose one opportunity to teach the Chinese that in Italy, we have *la Befana*, that the Christmas tree is a recent acquisition under the globalization influence, but that we rather have *il presepe* (Jesus crib) as a decoration, that our family reunion is held on the 24th of December, for a meal traditionally composed of all kinds of fish and seafood, etc., and I insist on the fact that Italy, though a very small country regarding its surface territory, holds several cultures and that what I am telling them may not be right in all of Italy, but in my own region.

I think we have not only the right but much more the duty to inform them on our own cultures and should not just say "thank you" when they offer us a stuffed Santa Claus on Dec. 25.

Nowadays, the Chinese have adopted Western fashion as well as the United States fast food. After almost 20 years in China, I'm still offered *xican* (Western food) when I'm a guest, and this means

MacDonald's or KFC! Or they order a coffee for me at dinner – a good Nescafe instant 2+1 coffee! – while they have tea, and a fruit salad covered with a whole jar of salad dressing because "this is what you foreigners like," they say... Or, in restaurants, the waiters change my chopsticks for a fork and a knife, willing to respect the difference. In fact, being the one from outside, isn't it up to me to adapt? But they do that with such good intentions and sincerity that they deserve an explanation.

The Chinese now celebrate Halloween, and think this is our *Qingming* (Day of the Dead), while it is a Celtic religious tradition that has become a social activity. If we come from a country where All Saints' Day is celebrated, on November 1, and/or the Day of the Dead, on November 2, why not tell them about our own culture, and explain how these days are celebrated, what we do on these occasions, comparing with their *Qingming* practices?

As the Chinese people like to get together, eat, sing, and dance, in other words, socialize and have fun, they don't miss one opportunity to do so. That's why they adopt all Western festivities, including Mother's Day, Father's Day, and Valentine's Day. They also do so because they feel it is "modern" while keeping their own celebrations such as Children's Day (June 1), Youth's Day (May 4), Teachers Day (September 10), Duanwu (or Dragon Boat festival on the 5th of the fifth Chinese Lunar month), and others*.

A Chinese reporter who writes for an English language paper published a good article about Tibet

Photo provided by Tobia Paolone.

but there were sound cultural mistakes. As I appreciate her and thought she deserved to be informed, I wrote her a letter. Here is an excerpt. "*...piling yak skulls and bones is a way for the Tibetans to offer prayers*," you wrote. Believers can do some acts such as piling stones for Lamaists, lighting a candle in church for Catholics, touching the ground with their forehead for Muslims; these are ways of worshipping. A prayer is something a believer "says" to God. He may speak from the bottom of his heart or recite prayers that have been written and memorized. Generally prayers serve to ask something from God (success for a child who is taking an exam, health for an ailing relative, the return of peace in wartime), or to chant the glory of God and thank the divinities. One can also offer a sacrifice to the gods, such as killing an animal and sharing the meat with the poor, but fruit, candies, and cakes placed in front of a statue in a temple are offerings, not sacrifices. Another point is using "Christian" synonymously with "Protestant," so the Chinese often say "Catholics and Christians," while the latter includes the former.

My readers and audience may fear being assimilated by the Chinese culture and prefer to stick to their own culture. Some have problems understanding the difference between integration and assimilation.

---

* For detailed information about Chinese and Western main holidays, refer to Carducci Lisa; *Pays en fêtes*, Beijing, China Intercontinental Press, 2009. French edition.

I think that if we really respect our original culture, we must deepen our knowledge of it, explain it, and spread it. The Chinese *jiaozi* are not *raviolis*. Italian pasta is not only *spaghetti*, so let's call it *pasta* and not *miantiao* (literally long noodles, meaning exclusively spaghetti). The tomato sauce (*salsa di pomodoro*) used to season Italian pasta has nothing to do with ketchup, and ketchup is American! Pizza is Italian, but not the one eaten at Pizza Hut, Domino's, etc.

When we have Chinese guests for dinner at home, they usually appreciate eating Western. But, as they are friends, not strangers, why not use this opportunity to show them how to hold, use, and deposit the forks, knives, and spoons? Who can teach them if we don't? They will really appreciate this "class" if it's done in a positive spirit.

Same when we hear a wild "Hôllôw!" shouted by a cab driver to eventual non-Chinese customers. I often tell them that the way they say it sounds like an insult. And I have taught many Chinese vendors that "Loo-ke-loo-ke" is not English, but a Chinese linguistic pattern based on the repetition of a verb to indicate a short action, *Kan yi kan*, and they were happy to learn to say "Have a look!"

Dining with Chinese friends is the best opportunity we have to exchange customs. Once, I was at one or my students' home where we had just arrived from Beijing after the end of the school term. Her mother told her in Chinese (which I didn't speak at that time, in 1993), "put your feet flat on the floor," and I saw the girl discreetly moving her legs, which had been crossed. Mine were, too, and I remembered reading that this position was not considered polite at the table. The mother had noticed that her daughter's shoulders were uneven, and surely had noticed mine as well. Recently, I was in a restaurant with eight Chinese in Inner Mongolia. At that time, I noticed that we all had our elbows on the table, and I laughed remembering how serious a breach of etiquette this was when I was young. And we discussed that. Times have changed...

Different culture, different vision

Different cultures mean different visions of things, and I would like to illustrate this point with three examples. There is an advertisement on TV where twin boys sitting on the living room carpet are playing with a toy which stops abruptly because the batteries are low on power. The boys take out the batteries and throw them over their shoulders. The mother says, "*Hei! Bie reng!* (Don't throw them!)" and the advertisement aims to say that the batteries still contain enough power to be used in the TV remote. I tested several Westerners on their first reaction to this advertisement. Just as I, they were expecting that the mother would educate her children on not throwing things on the floor but in the garbage can, or, in this case, in a special disposal container for used batteries.

Another example is when we talk about propaganda. The Chinese word for propaganda is *xuanchuan*, meaning literally "to spread information."

Yet, the West automatically reacts in a negative way to the "propaganda" of the communist/socialist culture countries, likening it to forgery, lie, brain washing, etc., and opposing it to its clean, open and straight "information." In a new perspective, since the end of the 1990s, I would say, the word "propaganda" is no longer used in China and has been replaced by terms such as public information or communications. China has changed, but the Western view on China has not necessarily followed. Moreover, when the United States promotes, for instance, the Obama political administration to young people, it's touted by some as only normal political "information," while a campaign launched by China to promote help to the Sichuan earthquake victims, in May 2008, was seen by some as just a "communist propaganda campaign." Biases don't belong exclusively to one or the other camp.

My last example is about education and examination systems in China. It could not be missed, as I have a 30-year teaching career behind me. Here I must make a distinction between North America and European countries when it comes to the West. Italy, for instance, stands between Canada and China regarding its educational concept.

The so-called thesis that the Chinese students write only once, at the end of their four years of university studies, is common homework in the Canada, even in primary school (from grade 4 as far as I know), and I am sad to say that, by what I have seen while teaching in China, most Chinese students' theses would be rejected in high schools in Canada for their lack of originality, scientific bases, and logical composition, and some published Chinese books would be refused by any editor.

Plagiarism or copying would absolutely disqualify a student's work in Canada, but, on the contrary, writings based only on imagination, without valid quotations or credits would not be considered serious work. About this astonishing aspect of the Chinese way of earning marks, serious measures have been taken against cheating in China, but the habit is still widespread. Moreover, parents, university administrations, students, and society in general often see cheating as normal in the process of getting a diploma, a post, or a title.

As exams in the Western world are a part of daily life, parents don't accompany their children to them, and many students don't feel much stress before an exam, while Chinese parents rent a hotel room for their children to prepare quietly, accompany them in taxis, and stand outside in the sun, praying, even fainting, exercising, and "keeping face" if their son or daughter (also preparing to keep face) leaves the examination hall without a huge smile.

In China, mothers especially are immobilized for two or three weeks before their children take the exams. They ask for a leave from work and stay home to prepare good meals for the poor kid who will play his future and the reputation of his family on the exam chessboard. For North Americans, such mothers are not admired but... rather ridiculous, while the American mothers who proceed with their normal activities during the exam periods of their children – a simple routine – are seen as heartless and looked down upon.

When I left Canada for China, my twin granddaughters were five months old. I was criticized by the Italian community for abandoning them and letting my daughter – their mother after all! – raise them by herself, while the only child in China is raised by two parents and four grandparents.

Once in China, I was blamed by Chinese mothers who had a different view on education. My granddaughters, then two years old, had come to visit me, and we were in a store where they saw a wide array of stuffed animals. The girls were entranced by the toys, and I let them admire and even caress them. Used to see things without buying, the girls didn't even ask me to buy the toys. But the observing women criticized me openly because I didn't buy any for my granddaughters.

Chinese babies don't cry because they are always in the arms of one or another adult. Crying is a good way to obtain anything they want, while most Western parents don't admit that a child uses the crying-and-shouting weapon to obtain satisfaction. Chinese children, grown up as chicks under the mother's wings, remain dependent on their parents even after marriage, while, by contrast, North American children, less controlled or under "remote control," are urged to develop independence, creativity, and freedom. These two opposite educational systems are blamed by their counterparts and praised by their followers.

"Da bai cai!"

How could I go away without a word on cabbage? I would say cabbage is the symbol of Chinese food culture. It was the vegetable of the poor in the past but also has an illustrious history. Easy to grow and keep, cabbage lends itself to any kind of preparation.

It was not so long ago when, during the first two weeks of November, every year, piles of cabbages sold as low as 3 *fen* (0.03 Yuan) per kilo. All around the city of Beijing, one could see trucks depositing their cabbages on the soil at street crossroads or in the work unit courtyards. Then, all kinds of carts and trolleys, bicycles and tricycles left, heavily loaded with the winter supply.

I asked several locals about the phenomenon, but almost all the residents I addressed had forgotten the

details, though we are talking of the very recent past.

For the winter months, families used to prepare salted vegetables in huge terracotta jars. Now that the fields transform into greenhouses at the beginning of winter, we can find all kinds of fresh vegetables all year round. Storage in the *siheyuan* courtyards and on the stairs of apartment buildings has almost disappeared. It has become useless to keep hundreds of kilos of *da bai cai* (big white vegetable) now. Do families who still store some on their balconies do it by romanticism? Though the tradition is no longer necessary, the image of piled cabbages still touches me and reminds me that hard but appreciated period of my Chinese life.

Conclusion

Now you know all my secrets. To be happy in China – and this is possible! – one has to be flexible, open, a good observer, and ready to adapt, as we have seen in these pages.

At the beginning of this book, I recalled a wise woman who said, "Every country has something good; why not look for what is good and continue to build on this value?" It is natural to be shocked by what represents a red light or crossroads on our way, and easier to be stricken by differences than by similarities. And it is the way we deal with such challenges and the solutions we choose that make the difference between a happy and unhappy life in China.

I would add a last point: the mirror. In 1989, I visited all kinds of stores to buy antiperspirant or deodorant. No way – this product didn't exist on the Chinese market. The first reaction of a Westerner was – as I noticed through the following years – that the Chinese don't have good hygiene habits. At that time, I was offered by a pharmacist

a medicine that he told me to apply once a week on my underarm. In fact, the Chinese underarm sweat glands are not developed, and, for them, an odor coming from this part of the body is the result of a disease.

Talking about smell, most Han Chinese like to eat *jiucai*, but chives have a strong smell we are not used to. Before criticizing the Chinese for this smell, unbearable at the beginning when we have just come to China and are not used to it, why not think that we also may have a smell they can't stand? When I arrived in Inner Mongolia recently, I found that the Mongols as well as the Hans and other ethnic groups had "a smell." It was due to their diet, which is essentially based on meat and dairy products. After more than one month in the region and, eating as they did, I didn't detect the smell anymore but, when I came back to Beijing, I realized that I had the same smell myself! It's then a good habit to reflect on ourselves the question we ask ourselves about others.

Do me a favor, be happy in China! This is the best I can wish for you and for China.

Lisa Carducci has been – cumulatively – a student for 21 years, a language teacher for 30 years, a journalist for 20, but a writer for her all life. Author of 67 books and 3,000 articles in a variety of languages, she has written mostly about China and the Chinese after she established in this country in 1991, following two visits in 1985 and 1989.

Born in Canada, she majored in Linguistics at the University of Montreal. In China she taught French and Italian in a Beijing university, worked with China Central Television (overseas service), and later with Beijing Review. Besides her career as a writer, she is an autodidact artist, with 20 exhibitions at her credit.

In 2001, Lisa Carducci was granted the Friendship Award of the People's Republic of China "for her outstanding contribution to the international friendship and her enthusiastic support to the construction of a modern China." In 2005, she was one of the first foreigners in China to be awarded the permanent residence in the PRC.

Several of her publications were awarded internationally.